COACHING

disabled performers

ISBN 1 902523 07 5

114 Cardigan Road
Headingley
Leeds LS6 3BJ
Tel: 0113-274 4802 Fax: 0113-275 5019
E-mail: coaching@sportscoachuk.org Website: www.sportscoachuk.org

Author: Annie Kerr
Editors: Penny Crisfield and Chris Rigg
Typesetter: Debbie Backhouse

Acknowledgements:
Geoff Smedley (Chair) and Peter Arnott, Barry Ginley, David McCrae,
Peter Neurauter, Mark Southam (members of the coaching sub-group of the
UK Coordinating Committee on sport for disabled people) and the
performers who gave their kind permission to use their personal profiles.
Sue Williams who typed the original manuscript.
John Clatworthy, Spencer Holmes, David Tillotson and Mahesh Patel of English Federation
of Disability Sport (EFDS) for their input.

Published on behalf of **sports coach UK** by
Coachwise Solutions
Chelsea Close
Off Amberley Road
Armley
Leeds LS12 4HP
Tel: 0113-231 1310 Fax: 0113-231 9606
E-mail: enquiries@coachwise.ltd.uk Website: www.1st4sport.com

Preface

If you are already coaching disabled performers or would like to do so, this pack is for you. As much of your existing coaching experience and knowledge is readily applicable to coaching disabled sportspeople, some basic coaching knowledge and experience is assumed. This comprehensive guide will help you to decide if, and how, you might need to adjust your coaching practice to meet their specific needs.

This home study pack builds on the information provided in the **sports coach UK (scUK)** Coaching Essentials resource and workshop *How to Coach Disabled People in Sport* and provides the supporting material for the **scUK** *Coaching Disabled Performers* workshop for those who want to further their coaching knowledge of working with disabled athletes. You are strongly recommended to enrol on the complementary workshop. All coaches are offered access to support and advice after the workshop. Workshop dates and locations are available from your Regional Training Unit (contact addresses and telephone numbers are available from **sports coach UK**).

Each chapter provides information, activities and questions to help you check your own understanding and apply it to your own sport. If the content is new to you, the study pack will take about 6–8 hours to complete (excluding the time taken to carry out the action plans at the end of each chapter).

All the biographical details in the performer profiles were correct at the time of first print. Please note that many performers will have progressed to new achievements in the interim.

Key to symbols used in the text

 An activity.

 Approximate length of time to be spent on the activity.

Contents

Introduction

1.0 What's in It for You?

You will probably have one aim in mind as you work through this study pack – to improve your ability to coach disabled performers. It is assumed you already have the necessary sport-specific coaching skills to Level Three or equivalent and are now seeking some additional knowledge and confidence. If you already adopt a coaching philosophy that focuses on building on the strengths and abilities of each individual, you will have no difficulty in meeting this new challenge. The pack will give you the necessary information, introduce you to a number of performers who have specific impairments and provide activities to help you apply everything to your sport and your own coaching.

Having worked through the pack, you should feel more confident and able to:

- apply and extend your existing coaching skills and experience to meet the needs of performers with a range of impairments[1]

- use appropriate terminology

- explain the benefits and issues of integrated and segregated sessions for different disability groups

- establish basic communication skills for coaching disabled performers

- identify appropriate safety and medical considerations

- direct performers to appropriate structures for competition (including classification systems)[2] and further coaching

- plan a coaching session for a disabled performer in your sport.

If you have already attended the **scUK** Coaching Essentials workshop *How to Coach Disabled People in Sport*, this will be an advantage – you will already have some awareness of types of impairments, effective communication and ways to adapt your coaching. You are also strongly encouraged to attend the taught workshop that accompanies this pack[3]. Some of the activities included in this pack ask you to collect information for further discussion at the workshop. This is important for your own development and understanding of working with athletes with disabilities.

If you have already coached disabled performers, you will be encouraged to use this experience as you work through the activities in the pack. If you have not, do not worry – you will be introduced to the stories and successes of eight disabled performers to give you a real insight and provide actual examples with which to work.

---

1   An impairment is a temporary or permanent loss of use of a faculty or part of the body.

2   Classification is a method of ensuring even and fair competition between disabled performers.

3   For further details, contact your nearest Regional Training Unit. Contact addresses and telephone numbers are available from **sports coach UK**.

In this first chapter, you will be encouraged to consider why disabled people choose to take part in sport, what skills and qualities coaches need to develop to work with them and how best to refer to their impairments.

1.1 Why Sport?

Before addressing issues about how to coach, it will be useful to stop and consider:

* why disabled people become involved in sport

* what makes a good coach, and in particular, a good coach of disabled performers.

The first activity encourages you to do this.

ACTIVITY I

1 In the left-hand top box list the reasons able-bodied performers take part in sport (you may wish to think of the performers you coach):

	Able-bodied Performers	Disabled Performers
Reasons		
Benefits		

2 In the right-hand top box, list the reasons why you think disabled performers take part in sport.

3 In the lower two boxes, suggest any further benefits sport might offer these individuals (eg weight loss and improved health).

4 Note any observations:

Now turn over.

1/2   *You probably found you listed the same in each of the top boxes, because the reasons why disabled people take part in sport are the same and just as wide ranging as for able-bodied performers. You may have listed reasons such as:*

- *to improve fitness*
- *to develop new skills*
- *to achieve in competition and perhaps gain recognition*
- *to make friends*
- *to experience a personal challenge*
- *to experience the thrill of competition*
- *for enjoyment.*

3   *You may also have recognised that sport can offer individuals a great deal more than simply an opportunity for participation, friendship, enjoyment and success. It can develop other skills that will enhance many areas of daily life. For example, improving confidence and self-esteem, learning how to take responsibility, handle pressure and stress, and cope with disappointments and setbacks as well as success. These are valuable skills for all people. They will be particularly important for disabled people who may gain greater independence as a result of increased fitness and mobility gained through participation in sport.*

How can the coach help people gain the potential benefits of sport? What skills and qualities are needed by the coach? Try Activity 2.

ACTIVITY 2

1 In the left-hand column, list the skills and qualities you feel are needed by a good coach:

Skills/Qualities of a Good Coach	Additional Skills/Qualities

2 In the right-hand column, list the additional skills and qualities you feel you would need to coach disabled performers. You may find this a bit difficult at this stage but if you try it again after you have completed the study pack, you will feel more confident in your answers.

Now turn over.

1   *Coaches are all different – they have different qualities, bring different skills and experiences, and coach in different ways. However, you may have been able to identify some skills and qualities you feel are very important, such as the ability to:*

- *communicate effectively – to ask questions, give and receive information, provide feedback*
- *plan and organise sessions and programmes to meet the needs of performers*
- *analyse and evaluate performance to gauge and direct progress*
- *create a safe environment*
- *be open-minded in developing coaching skills and knowledge[1].*

2   *In addition, in the right-hand column, you may have included:*

- *a broad knowledge of an individual performer's impairment*
- *an in-depth knowledge of the individual performer you are coaching*
- *a knowledge of the competition classifications that operate in disabled sport (Chapter Five provides further information)*
- *information regarding specialised equipment*
- *a knowledge of the relevant safety and medical implications of working with specific impairment groups.*

You have probably realised the answers you have given are very similar (or even the same) whether or not you are considering disabled participants. All coaching is about helping people to be better – better at sport and better in life in general. It is about identifying the needs of each individual and helping them to achieve their aspirations. Coaching disabled performers is no different and this pack will continue to reinforce this point.

1.2   Terminology

Terminology can create problems. What is acceptable? How should you refer to a disability or a disabled person? What do disabled people prefer? Disabled people will have an individual, personal way of referring to their own disability.

Some definitions of disability have been based on a medical model (ie generalisations based on the medical condition such as everyone with Down's syndrome[2] is overweight). However, these have largely been rejected by disabled people as they focus on what disabled people **cannot** do, rather on what they **can** do. The social model of disability points out that the environment, social systems and people's attitudes are in fact what disable people. It is better to think about what disabled people can do and not about the medical label for their condition. This will enable you to provide a positive, welcoming coaching environment.

---

1   For further information, you are recommended to attend the **scUK** Coach Workshop *Coaching Methods and Communication* and read the handbook *The Successful Coach: Guidelines for Coaching Practice* (complimentary with the workshop). All **scUK** resources are available from **Coachwise 1st4sport** (0113-201 5555).

2   This is a congenital condition caused by chromosome abnormality. For further information, see Appendix A.

Be careful with terminology. For example use *people with cerebral palsy* (not *spastics*), *people with a learning disability* (not *the mentally handicapped*) and *wheelchair users* (not *wheelchairs*). If you feel uncomfortable with a term, discuss it with the individual, but never assume what is acceptable to one performer is acceptable to another, even if they have similar impairments.

1.3 Recap and Action Plan

The activities and advice in this chapter are intended to increase your interest, enthusiasm and confidence to coach disabled performers. The next chapter will continue to build your confidence and knowledge and give you an opportunity to practise adapting your coaching skills to the needs of disabled performers.

ACTION PLAN

If you want to coach disabled performers, you need to understand them as people who enjoy sport. If you already know someone, this action plan will be easy. If you do not, you will need to find one or more disabled persons actively involved in a sport – observe, speak to them and find out what sport means to them; talk about your sport with them. If you have difficulty locating people, contact your English Federation of Disability Sport Regional Manager or your home country/regional sports council – addresses in Appendix E.

Make a note of your observations and feelings:

Notes

Providing Sports Opportunities

2.0 What's in It for You?

This chapter looks at the different sporting opportunities available to disabled performers and then at some of the factors you would need to take into consideration when you provide these different opportunities. It will also help you identify the skills you will need to support disabled performers in their chosen sports. You will realise that disability sport is organised in a different way from able-bodied sport.

Do not worry if it initially seems confusing. The pack will help unravel the complexities and guide you to appropriate organisations for further advice (see Appendix E). In this way, you will be better equipped to advise and direct your performers to appropriate activities and organisations. By the end of this chapter, you should be able to:

- explain the benefits and issues of integrated and segregated sessions for different disability groups

- explain how inclusion offers more than integration

- identify the factors you would need to consider and apply if a disabled sportsperson wanted to be coached by you or wanted to compete in your sport.

You will also be introduced to two disabled performers in this chapter (Tanni and Marsha) and encouraged to consider whether and how you might accommodate them in your coaching sessions.

Is it possible? What might you need to do? The activities may also challenge any predetermined ideas you might have regarding sport for disabled people.

2.1 Levels of Participation

The model in Figure 1 will help you understand the opportunities available to disabled performers.

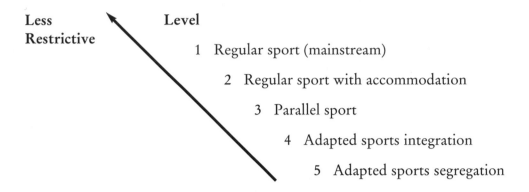

Less Restrictive

Level

1 Regular sport (mainstream)

2 Regular sport with accommodation

3 Parallel sport

4 Adapted sports integration

5 Adapted sports segregation

Figure 1: The Winnick Model
Adapted from Winnick, PJ (1987) *An Integration Continuum for Sports Participation*
Adapted Physical Activity Quarterly, Vol 4 (3) 158

This model was developed by Winnick in 1987 to show the different levels at which disabled performers could train and compete.

Level 1: regular sport (mainstream)

Total integration (coaching, competition and social) of disabled performers into mainstream competition and clubs (eg an athlete with a learning disability training, competing and socialising in a local athletics club).

Level 2: regular sport with accommodation

Integration of disabled performers into regular competition, clubs and coaching with some flexibility in the rules and regulations to enable integration and equal opportunities to non-disabled peers (eg wheelchair tennis players and able-bodied tennis players playing up and down doubles where wheelchair players are allowed two bounces of the ball).

Level 3: parallel sport

Disabled performers competing in the same event as their able-bodied peers but in their own section (eg wheelchair athletes in a marathon).

Level 4: adapted sports integration

Disabled and able-bodied performers participating in an adapted sport, in a segregated setting (eg forming teams for the purposes of developing a wheelchair basketball competition).

Level 5: adapted sports segregation

Disabled performers competing in a competition solely for that particular disability group (eg goalball[1]).

Disabled performers can be accommodated at various levels of the Winnick continuum depending on factors such as:

- individual choice
- level of ability
- type of sport
- opportunities available to the performer.

Performers could also be at different levels in Winnick's continuum for different purposes. For example they might:

- compete at Level 1 locally but aim for elite competition at Level 5
- train at Level 1 but compete at Levels 3 and 5
- compete at Levels 1 or 2 in one sport, or Levels 3 or 5 in another
- compete at Level 5 and coach at Levels 1 and 5.

2.2 Segregation, Integration and Inclusion

To what extent should disabled performers be **integrated** into mainstream sport and when should they be **segregated**? This is a difficult question because you need to weigh up a number of issues such as the:

- type of sport – some sports are readily accessible and individual, so integration is relatively easy (eg archery, swimming)
- views of the disabled performer – some prefer to train and compete only with other disabled participants, others prefer to be fully integrated
- views of the coach – his/her ability and willingness to adapt and organise sessions appropriately to facilitate integration
- views of other participants – they may feel they are not getting sufficient attention or their training needs are not being fully met, if programmes have been adapted to allow disabled performers to be fully integrated
- views of uninformed others – such as parents and helpers who may question the appropriateness of integrating a disabled performer into the session (social change often encounters resistance initially).

---

1 Goalball is an indoor ball game which is played by visually impaired people on a tactile court using a ball with a bell in it.

You also need to recognise there are many forms and degrees of **integration.** In some cases, it can mean playing together, sharing a facility, joint membership of a club, events for disabled people in governing body championships, joint squad training or the recruitment of disabled people as staff, committee members, officials and coaches. **Inclusion** means that all performers can have an opportunity to participate in sport at a suitable level with appropriate support. Disabled performers can often be integrated but not necessarily included. The following activity will help you gain a better understanding of this.

ACTIVITY 3

1   Read through the following personal profile.

> *Tanni Grey, MBE[1]*
>
> *Aged 27, Tanni is an elite track athlete. She trains six days a week, 50 weeks of the year in a variety of situations. She pushes[2] 60–140 miles each week including track and hill sessions as well as weight training. She also swims and plays recreational wheelchair tennis. In the 1996 Paralympics, Tanni won one gold medal for the 800m and three silver medals for the 100m, 200m and 400m events. She also won four gold medals in the 1994 World Championships in Berlin. Tanni's aspirations are to carry on competing and to achieve for as long as possible. Tanni is the Disability Coordinator for the BT athletics programme based at the British Athletic Federation headquarters in Birmingham. Tanni has spina bifida[3] and uses a wheelchair.*

---

1   Bibliographic details correct at the time of publication.

2   Pushes refers to the way the wheelchair is self-propelled.

3   Spina bifida is a condition in which individuals are born with a defect in the vertebral column. Appendix A provides more information.

2 In the left-hand column, list the factors you would need to consider if Tanni wanted coaching in your sport:

Coaching	Competition

3 In the right-hand column, note all the factors you would have to consider if Tanni wanted to compete in your sport.

4 Using the Winnick model on page 10, determine which sporting opportunity/ies would be most appropriate for Tanni if she wanted to take up your sport:

Now turn over.

1 *Some of the factors you would need to consider before Tanni joined your coaching group might include one or more of the following:*

- *Which activities has Tanni done previously?*

- *What are her aspirations in the sport?*

- *What are appropriate warm-ups? As Tanni is a wheelchair user, you may need to include different activities.*

- *Can Tanni attend coaching sessions alongside able-bodied performers? This will depend on such factors as access to facilities (ramps etc).*

- *Would she need a personal programme?*

For example in swimming and field athletics, Tanni could be coached alongside her able-bodied peers. In team games, such as basketball or hockey, Tanni could be coached alongside able-bodied peers for part of a session but may need more skill-specific coaching (eg pushing, dribbling, passing) and tactics that would be slightly different from her peers as she is a wheelchair user. A good coach will be able to accommodate the individual needs of a performer with a bit of innovative thinking.

2 *If Tanni wanted to compete in your sport, you would need to consider:*

- *the opportunities available at local, regional, national and international levels (see Chapter Five)*

- *whether rules or equipment could be adapted to accommodate Tanni. For example in wheelchair tennis, players are allowed two bounces of the ball. It may be possible for Tanni to play singles or doubles matches.*

3 *Tanni could be coached at wheelchair tennis on a sessional basis and compete in both local and high level competition. Tanni could be coached in track and field at club level but also compete in national and international competitions. In sailing, Tanni might have access to a range of coaching and competition opportunities ranging from local to international level.*

4 *You may have suggested that Tanni would not be suited to your sport or patently could not participate however much adaptation was made (eg it would be impossible to take part in the high jump).*

2.3 Factors Affecting Participation

Don't make too many assumptions about whether performers can participate in your sport, for you will be surprised how easily sports can be adapted and how many disabled performers can be successful with a positive and willing coach. This pack will help you find ways to adapt your coaching. Try the next activity.

ACTIVITY 4

1 Meet Marsha by reading through the following profile:

> **Marsha Cooper[1]**
> *Marsha, aged 50, is a civil servant and lives on the Wirral. She is a keen sailor and sails dinghies and cruisers as often as she can. Marsha has a visual impairment[2]. Her achievements to date include gaining her Royal Yachting Association Dinghy Levels 1 and 2, competing in the World Blind Regatta in New Zealand where she helmed a 10m keelboat, and cruising and racing a variety of inshore and offshore craft. Marsha's aspirations for the future are to continue dinghy and offshore cruising and to promote visually impaired sailing through RYA Sailability.*

2 Consider how Marsha could take part in your sport and give your reasons:

3 List some of the factors you would need to consider:

Now turn over.

---

1 Bibliographic details correct at time of publications.

2 In this pack, the term visual impairment refers to those who are totally blind as well as those who are partially sighted. There are many eye conditions. Do not make assumptions about your performer's visual impairment and abilities.

If a visually impaired athlete aspires to compete at international level, for example pole vaulting, hurdles or steeplechase, it is important for the coach to make them aware that there are currently no Paralympic competitions in these disciplines. Contact the British Paralympic Association for further information on Paralympic events (Appendix E).

Some of the factors will be the same as those you considered for Tanni – for example, adapting rules or using special equipment. You may have decided that Marsha could not participate in your sport – for example, it would be difficult for her to play hockey or netball. However, Marsha may be able to take part in skills training sessions, small games (with appropriate equipment and adapted rules) and fitness training sessions. Other sports such as archery, bowls, athletics and swimming may pose few or no problems for Marsha. You may still feel it is impossible for performers with a visual impairment like Marsha to be coached in your sport. However, remember that very few visually impaired people are totally blind, and by communicating with the performer, you will be able to establish his/her level of vision and what can realistically be achieved.

However, the performer may wish to be coached in those sports simply because he/she enjoys them. All that may be needed is to consider the safety factors and perhaps a guide to talk the performer through activities and describe where to position him/herself in relation to targets.

Performers with disabilities and their coaches can work together in a positive way to adapt rules and equipment to accommodate their needs. Of course there are occasions when a disabled performer will be unable to take part in a particular sport – for example hurdling for a wheelchair user. This point is considered further at the workshop.

2.4 Role of the Coach

In order to provide sports opportunities for disabled performers, it is your responsibility to become as familiar as possible with the needs of individual performers and the requirements of your sport – particularly about the rules and equipment for disabled performers. This can be achieved by making contact with the appropriate disability sports organisation, your sport-specific governing body and, of course, talking to the performers themselves. This will help you become familiar with any safety requirements associated with the performer's impairment. Coaches need to be encouraged to think about the most effective way of communicating with their athletes, whatever the impairment. This area is covered in greater detail in Chapters Three and Five and Appendices A and C.

Planning for success in competition and training will be motivating for you as well as your performers. If it is not possible for the performer to measure success by winning a competition, set achievable goals in training by which success can be measured. Chapter Five on competition may help you to do this. By liaising with local and regional clubs and associations, you may be able to find further opportunities for competition within existing structures. If there are no opportunities available, you may be able to introduce competition for disabled performers as part of existing structures.

You may be able to identify other roles for coaches to play in providing sports opportunities for disabled performers. They are probably similar, if not identical to those needed to work with able-bodied performers. The National Disability Sports Organisations (NDSO), sport-specific national governing bodies (NGB) and other structures mentioned in Appendix E will be able to offer support and guidance if required. Regional development coordinators may provide good contacts if the sport has them. You will also gain further help through attendance at the taught workshop.

2.5 Recap and Action Plan

The information in this chapter should give you an idea of the range of opportunities you can provide for disabled performers. You may have realised that it is often easier to provide coaching opportunities for individual performers than to identify appropriate opportunities for competition. This is dealt with again in Chapter Five. The next chapter looks in more detail at how you can adapt your coaching skills to meet the specific needs of disabled performers.

ACTION PLAN

In the first chapter, you were encouraged to talk with disabled performers. Now you are asked to find someone who already coaches disabled performers. If you have difficulty, contact your national governing body.

Find out from the coach:

- why he/she coaches disabled people:

- how he/she got started:

- what difficulties he/she has encountered and how these were dealt with:

- what satisfaction and enjoyment he/she gains:

Start to think about who you might coach and make some notes to help you get started. For example, your sport might be suited to disabled performers with a particular impairment, or you may have a special interest in coaching performers with a particular impairment (you may already know one or be coaching one).

Notes

Safety and Medical Considerations

3.0　What's in It for You?

An awareness of safety is paramount in all coaching sessions and competitions, irrespective of whether there are disabled or able-bodied participants. Similarly all coaches need to be aware of any personal conditions which may influence what is included in the session or how it is managed.

This chapter contains basic information for coaches about how to provide safe sport for all performers. You will be encouraged to consider the:

- same safety and personal factors you would assess for non-disabled performers
- importance of treating each performer as a unique individual – as you should in all coaching situations.

There may seem to be a lot of new and perhaps rather technical or medical information in this chapter. Don't worry – you will have plenty of opportunities to return to this chapter later in the pack and start to use the information. In this way, it will begin to have some real meaning in your coaching. Whatever your experience in working with disabled sportspeople, by the end of this chapter you should be able to:

- reflect on your current practice with regard to safety and personal factors and identify the key factors
- adapt your coaching practice to work effectively and safely with disabled performers.

In subsequent chapters, you will have the opportunity to put this knowledge into practice as you design and organise coaching sessions and plan for competitions.

3.1 General Considerations

The first activity in the pack (page 3) provided an opportunity for reflection as well as perhaps a reminder about good coaching practice. The next one asks you to consider how you ensure safety in your current coaching situation.

ACTIVITY 5

1 In the left-hand column, list the safety factors you would consider when coaching able-bodied performers:

General Safety Factors	Additional Factors

2 In the right-hand column, add any additional factors or modifications that you believe would be important when working with disabled performers (you may choose to do this for one particular group of disabled performers or generally).

Now turn over.

Compare your answers with the following list regarding general safety factors:

- *Knowledge of performers with conditions such as epilepsy[1], asthma, diabetes, anaemia, hay fever and how they manage their conditions.*

- *Factors relating to conditioning, new or old injuries and fatigue, so you can recognise their effect when a performer is training.*

- *Number of people using a venue and the activities they are doing.*

- *The weather and temperature, the need for fluid replacement.*

- *Location of first aid equipment and first aid personnel.*

- *Specific hazards and safety precautions associated with your sport. For example moving in front of a javelin throwing area while a performer is throwing.*

- *Evacuation procedures due to emergencies (eg for fire).*

There are additional factors to consider when working with disabled performers to ensure a safe environment and coaching practice. These are explained in the next section so you can check your answers as you read. Remember, disabled performers will be well aware of their own individual safety and personal needs. However, each person will have individual ways of dealing with personal and safety considerations. This may often depend on whether the disability has been acquired or whether the performer was born with it. For example, an amputee[2] who has lost a limb through an accident may have scar tissue that will need protection, whereas an athlete born without a limb may not have scar tissue.

Other factors you might need to consider include the possibility that some disabled performers may:

- *tire more quickly and so need shorter work intervals with longer rests*

- *find it harder to concentrate – for example, a visually impaired swimmer in a noisy pool*

- *experience poor balance and coordination and so may be prone to injuries from falling, dropping objects or knocking against things*

- *need extra safety considerations for emergency evacuation as well as for access (eg there should be visual warnings as well as auditory ones for fire or bomb warnings)*

- *need to be lifted (eg those using wheelchairs) to transfer from a wheelchair to the floor. Coaches are advised not to do any lifting or handling, but need to understand the transfer technique for instructional purposes. Contact your local health authority, who will be able to provide a contact in your area. Coaches should also ask the performers themselves, as they will also be able to give advice.*

---

1   Epilepsy is a tendency to have recurrent seizures due to an altered chemical state within the brain.

2   The term amputee refers to individuals who have at least one major joint missing or no functional movement remaining in the joint through which the amputation has been made.

Don't worry if there seem to be lots of extra things to think about – you will have a chance to use this information again in subsequent chapters. Although the disabled performers will probably not need to be told how to look after themselves, it is important for coaches to understand their needs and provide for them during training and competition.

3.2 Specific Considerations

In this section, you will find some specific considerations pertinent to particular types of impairment. Check your answers to the second part of Activity 5 as you read.

Amputee performers

Some amputee performers use a **prosthesis**[1]. An everyday prosthesis, as the name suggests, is not designed to withstand the pressures of training and competition, so performers should be advised to see a prosthetist to have a sports modified prosthesis. Advanced technology and materials ensure that a prosthesis is strong and lightweight. Some artificial knee joints have a built in computers and artificial feet are made from carbon fibre. to allow the performer to move in a similar way to that of a natural limb or joint. If a prosthesis fails (it splits or breaks) it could injure a performer, so coaches need to ensure the performer:

- checks that the prosthesis is suitable for the sport
- regularly checks the prosthesis for signs of wear
- is aware that it may take some time to get used to a new prosthesis
- responds to complaints of soreness in the lower back, by referring to the prosthetist to check length and weight[2].

Amputee performers have greater difficulty **regulating body temperature** because the ratio of surface area to body volume is different and could result in overheating. Coaches must therefore ensure performers wear suitable clothing and ample opportunities are provided for rehydration and recovery.

It is important to take good care of the **stump** – the stump sock (worn over the stump to protect it) needs to be changed regularly as it can produce soreness or become slippery if covered in sweat. If the stump becomes blistered, the performer will miss out on training or competition. The stump should be checked regularly by the performer and any breaks of skin treated to avoid infection and allow healing. It may be necessary to organise alternative training to allow the stump to heal. If the prosthesis is rubbing the stump, refer the performer to the prosthetist.

---

1   Artificial replacement for a limb of the body.

2   Refer to the British Amputee and Les Autres Sports Association (BALASA) for advice from a prosthetist with specific knowledge of sport.

Performers with cerebral palsy

Cerebral palsy is not a disease or illness. It is a brain lesion which is non-progressive and causes variable impairment of the coordination, tone and strength of muscle action impacting on postures and movement. The degree of impairment between individuals with cerebral palsy varies considerably according to the severity and site of the brain damage. No two people with cerebral palsy are alike because the brain damage that causes the condition can evolve differently in each individual. You may not be very familiar with this condition, so it may help to meet Dean first before considering the particular safety issues of which you need to be aware.

> *Dean Thomas[1]*
> *Dean, aged 25, is the Development Officer for the National Boccia Federation[2]. He plays boccia and was a member of the British Paralympic Team in Atlanta. He is especially interested in developing the coaching and refereeing side of boccia. As a performer with cerebral palsy, Dean sometimes experiences inflammation in his right knee and left shoulder. This results from overuse of these two limbs. Dean also has periods of spasm (this is often connected with cerebral palsy). To increase general fitness and relax overworked limbs and spasm, he swims regularly and does exercises such as rolling. Dean uses a battery powered wheelchair for mobility. His aspirations for the future include winning gold medals at the Paralympics and continuing to play boccia.*

Performers with cerebral palsy may be prone to **accidents and injuries** because they have problems with balance and coordination. For example, in throwing events, the projectile may be inadvertently dropped on a foot. The types of injuries that performers with cerebral palsy may acquire will depend on the nature of the disability. For example, ambulant[3] performers will have different considerations (ie their legs) from performers who use wheelchairs, who will need to consider their upper body requirements.

Performers with cerebral palsy may also suffer more frequently from **dehydration, muscle cramps** and **exhaustion.** If, because of their mobility, performers rely on assistants to help them to drink, they may not take in enough fluids. This also has implications where there is reliance on an assistant for other purposes – for example, to apply suncream. Some performers with moderate to mild dysfunction may experience muscle cramps in hot weather. Coaches and assistants therefore need to take extra precautions in hot weather and during hard training sessions, you need to know what signs to look for (ie rate of perceived exertion). Similarly, if there is poor motor efficiency, performers will be more prone to exhaustion after intense effort. As a coach you should be aware of this and monitor drills and training schedules accordingly.

Some performers with cerebral palsy may also be more susceptible to common illnesses (eg colds and flu), as well as having other medical conditions such as epilepsy and respiratory difficulties – they may have difficulty exhaling and particular care should therefore be taken when swimming. Because of the nature of cerebral palsy, some athletes may have a learning disability or appear slow in speech or aural comprehension.

---

1   Biographical details correct at the time of publication.

2   Boccia is a game similar to boules or petanque played to Paralympic level.

3   Non-wheelchair users.

Performers with a learning disability

A learning disability is a condition where a performer's brain does not develop as fast or as fully as someone with no learning disability. The degree of learning disability can vary enormously. A learning disability can be caused by several factors but the most common are:

- **genetic** – inherited characteristic, such as in people with Down's syndrome
- **infection** – such as the result of contracting meningitis
- **traumatic** – for example, from an accident at birth, physical abuse as a baby or from an accident, such as a road traffic accident
- **social** – for example, as a result of pre-natal influences such as drugs, alcohol, smoking, malnutrition and pollution
- **vaccine damage** – for example, reaction to whooping cough vaccine.

To qualify for international competition, individuals with a learning disability will have an IQ of 75 or below.

As a coach, you should ensure your performers understand the specific safety rules associated with your sport. Situations that appear to be an obvious danger may not be perceived as such by some individuals with a learning disability. Accidents may occur due to the lack of awareness of the imminent danger of a situation or the inability to respond appropriately and swiftly if given a command. Some athletes may have relatively poor self-care skills and will need guidance (from you or assistants) in areas such as:

- avoidance of sunburn, exhaustion and dehydration – they may need to be reminded frequently to drink or use sun barrier creams (be aware – some medication can make skin more sensitive to the sun)
- appropriate clothing – is an outfit too hot, too cold, does footwear fit adequately, is an outfit suitable for the sport?

Performers with a learning disability are also more likely than their able-bodied peers to have convulsive disorders such as epilepsy (see Appendix B).

Performers with a visual impairment

You have already met Marsha (page 15) who has a visual impairment. When coaching visually impaired athletes, it is useful to remember the following basic points with regard to safety:

- Do not leave equipment lying on the floor – always try to leave it in the same place each session so performers know where it is.
- Allow performers time to orientate themselves in a venue and pinpoint any potential dangers such as slippery areas, doorways and obstacles. Alternatively, avoid these areas altogether.
- Be aware of any changes in the environment that could cause an injury, such as open doors, cupboards, windows, discarded kit or even someone walking into an open space unannounced.
- Reduce or be aware of any background noise.
- Ensure that guides for runners are briefed properly so that athletes have an understanding of what is happening around them; in the case of experienced guides this will be a matter of routine.
- Sighted athletes must be aware of visually impaired athletes as they have a responsibility to ensure their safety.

Some specific medical conditions need extra considerations:

- Performers with a **detached retina**[1] could be at risk of further detachment if they experience blows to the head. Generally speaking, therefore, these performers should avoid contact sports and gain medical advice regarding safe activities.

- Performers suffering from **glaucoma**[2] should gain medical advice regarding activities which require exertion, such as power lifting.

Performers who are deaf or hard of hearing

Communication difficulties can result in accidents. Coaches must give sufficient time to ensure that deaf performers fully understand safety regulations and procedures. Balance and coordination can be affected. It is useful if venues have a visual stimulus as well as a fire alarm and staff are aware that deaf (or visually impaired) performers are in the venue.

Wheelchair performers

You have already met Tanni (page 12) and will have the opportunity to meet another wheelchair user in Chapter Four (page 38). People with a variety of impairments use wheelchairs – some only need to use them sometimes but others may need them all the time to carry out their activities for daily living.

The following basic points apply to performers who are paraplegic and tetraplegic[3]. You will find some additional points that refer specifically to performers with tetraplegia:

- Paralysis affects the body's ability to perspire below the site of the lesion, so **overheating** may occur. Therefore, performers should be encouraged to drink regularly, seek shade between drills or events when training, wear light clothing and use spray bottles to cool off. Performers with tetraplegia are even more susceptible to temperature regulation problems.

- Some performers may have relatively **poor circulation** so need to change their sitting position regularly to encourage blood flow. Poor circulation may also cause dizziness. As circulation is even poorer in performers with tetraplegia, dizzy spells may be more frequent. An elasticated corset worn around the upper stomach and lower rib cage can help to reduce dizziness as can breathing deeply and changing posture. Athletes may have difficulty in achieving aerobic exercise due to dependence on smaller upper muscle groups. Stabilisation is often required when the athlete stops.

- Wheelchair users are prone to **pressure sores** because of poor circulation and movement restrictions. They should be encouraged to watch out for signs of pressure sores (eg redness, inflammation, skin breaking down) and take preventative care (eg massage, change of position, cushioning, protecting, medical advice). Pressure sores take longer to heal because of poor circulation and could affect a performer's training and competition schedule.

---

1   This involves the detachment of the light sensitive layer at the back of the eye on which the incoming light rays are focused.

2   This occurs when there is an abnormally high amount of fluid in the eyeball which exerts pressure onto the retina and the optic nerve. This can eventually lead to blindness.

3   Paraplegia refers to paralysis of the lower part of the body. Tetraplegia refers to paralysis of all four limbs. For more information see Appendix A.

As a coach, you should be aware that some wheelchair performers will use special appliances or procedures to compensate for loss of **bowel or bladder** control. Usually, the only requirements for performers are privacy and adequate facilities for carrying out necessary personal procedures. However, you should be aware that some personal procedures will need to be continued during a training programme or competition so these needs must be accommodated.

Occasionally accidents occur because performers are unable to feel sensation in their limbs. They could, for example, scrape toes or feet if they are dragged across the bottom of a swimming pool, or be damaged when using equipment if adequate padding is not provided. Other accidents, such as hand blistering as a result of pushing, and cuts and scrapes from wheels can usually be avoided through adequate taping of the fingers and the use of padded gloves.

Performers with tetraplegia may suffer from decreased breathing efficiency because the diaphragm muscle may be the only respiratory muscle that remains in working order. This sometimes affects the ability to cough and clear the airway, so infections are more likely to occur. Exercise can improve the development of muscles in the neck that can improve breathing efficiency. If a chest or breathing difficulty is noticed, the performer should always seek medical advice.

Performers with tetraplegia may suffer from automatic dysreflexia[1] which can result in high blood pressure, sweating, chills and headaches. If a performer is unable to feel there is something wrong because of lack of sensation, these reactions will be the first indication of a problem elsewhere in the body. It is important to try to find the cause of the reaction by ensuring that bladders are able to empty freely and there are no obvious sites of injury. If this does not help a performer recover, seek immediate medical advice.

Performers with spina bifida

Tanni (page 12) has spina bifida. The same considerations should be taken into account as for performers with paraplegia. However, if the performer has hydrocephalus[2], he or she may have a shunt[3] fitted. It is important to take care not to displace the shunt when the athlete is being lifted or transferred. Activities such as heading a football should also be avoided. If a performer complains of headaches, nausea and dizziness, it is wise to seek medical advice to ensure the shunt is working properly. There is a high incidence of allergy to latex/rubber, which needs to be considered with balloon-based activities.

---

1   Automatic dysreflexia or hyperflexia is a reaction of parts of the body to various stimuli which are outside conscious control. For example, an over extended bladder or a limb which has been kept in a painful position can trigger a reaction.

2   Hydrocephalus is an accumulation of cerebrospinal fluid in the brain that makes it swell. For more information see Appendix A.

3   Shunts are inserted into the cranium to remove excess cerebrospinal fluid. For more information see Appendix A.

3.3 Recap and Action Plan

The information in this chapter is intended as a guide to some of the safety and personal/medical issues coaches need to consider. It is always preferable to discuss specific requirements with individual performers to ensure their needs are understood. If you require more information on any of the contents of this chapter, you are recommended to contact the appropriate national disability sports organisations or the relevant disability organisation (addresses in Appendix E).

ACTION PLAN

If you already know a disabled performer, go back and read again all the safety and medical issues regarding his/her specific impairment. If you do not yet know a disabled performer, select one of the disabled participants already introduced in this pack (ie Tanni, Marsha or Dean). Make a note of all the factors with which you should be particularly concerned but remember that every person is different. Some individuals may have further problems (eg a visually impaired athlete may be deaf as well). Make full use of Appendices A and B:

• Individual:

• Impairment:

• Factors for concern:

Implications for Coaching

4.0 What's in It for You?

This chapter will help you identify how you can adapt your coaching to meet the needs of specific disabled performers. You will be introduced to four more performers and given the opportunity to undertake a series of activities that will involve these performers (or others that you know) and your own sport. By the end of the chapter, you should be able to:

- describe how to adapt your communication skills and coaching style to meet the needs of individual performers

- plan coaching sessions for performers in an integrated setting and on an individual basis

- identify key points for working with performers with sensory impairments, physical disabilities, learning disabilities and/or a combination of these.

4.1 Communication and Coaching Style

A key element of successful coaching is effective communication – this means giving and receiving information. Both are equally important. How you communicate and the way you build relationships with your performers determine your coaching style. Some coaches do a lot of telling and showing, good coaches also do plenty of questioning and listening. You may find there are additional challenges to how you coach and the way you communicate when coaching disabled performers.

Giving information

Information can be shared in many ways – speaking is the most common but do not underestimate the impact of non-verbal communication such as gestures, expressions and even posture. The latter can be more powerful than the actual words spoken – it is suggested that 90% of information is actually conveyed non-verbally. Of course, non-verbal forms of communication can become **the** form of communication for those with hearing impairments. Most coaches are good at giving information but remember it is important to give not just relevant information but an appropriate amount and in the right way (ie in terms of tone and pitch as well as the actual words chosen and the complexity). Too much information can lead to boredom, misunderstanding and even frustration and this may be particularly true if there are challenges to communication – for example those with a learning disability, speech or hearing impairment. Too negative feedback can reduce self-confidence, progress and enjoyment. Coaches must be careful not to demonstrate poor practice (eg 'don't do it this way') as often people who are relying on non-verbal communication will assume that the demonstration is of good practice.

Gaining information

Compared with information giving skills, coaches often tend to be relatively poor at asking good questions and really listening to what performers have to say. Coaches can learn a great deal about their performers, their strengths and weaknesses, hopes and fears, if they listen to them and ask questions.

The use of open questions (ie those which demand a response other than simply yes or no) is important in any coaching environment but it is particularly valuable when coaching disabled performers – they all have very individual needs and goals. It is too easy to make assumptions about what they want or what they can and cannot do. Always ask so you really get to know each athlete and build a good relationship with him/her.

Again coaches working with disabled performers may need to become particularly skilled at a variety of different methods of communication – different ways of giving information by telling, showing and guiding; different ways of gaining information by listening, watching and asking. You could ask performers how you can make an activity more challenging. Coaching disabled athletes requires a great deal of patience and understanding. The next sections point out some of the special skills required.

Visually impaired performers

The next activity will help you think through the challenges you may face when working with visually impaired performers.

ACTIVITY 6

1   Read again the personal profile of Marsha, page 15. It is important to realise there are many different eye conditions. Do not make general assumptions about your performer's visual impairment and abilities. Appreciate that some environmental factors might affect the individual's performance – for example lighting, use of colour, noise reverberations. It is also important to remember to give very clear instructions and avoid non-verbal communication. These points will be enlarged upon later in this section.

2   If you are coaching Marsha in your own sport, list what you would need to consider and perhaps adapt in order to ensure successful communication:

Now turn over.

Performers with a visual impairment can usually be coached in a similar way to their sighted peers. As a coach, you need sound sport-specific knowledge and the ability to communicate this knowledge effectively to the performer. However, you may have listed the following in your answer:

- *Although she is visually impaired, does Marsha have any sight? If so, how much?*

- *Always address Marsha by name and state your own name.*

- *Do not walk away from Marsha without telling her.*

- *You may need to use touch but always establish touching protocols. Coaches need to be aware of child protection issues when working with young athletes.*

- *Use key words – for example, avoid long complicated sentences and focus on a few words that convey what you are trying to say.*

- *Be logical and sequential when presenting information.*

- *Ensure verbal instructions are concise, accurate and understood. If she does not understand instructions, she may not be able to copy sighted performers.*

- *Be aware of the influence of environmental factors that can influence how you communicate. For example:*
  - *the amount of available light*
  - *changes in light (cloud cover)*
  - *type of light (sun, fluorescent lights, floodlights)*
  - *positioning of performer and/or coach in relation to light source*
  - *level of background noise (echo or reverberation, ventilation fans).*

  Establish with Marsha how these can affect her during coaching sessions and competition.

Initially it may be useful to enlist the help of someone familiar with Marsha to assist her in coaching sessions; they would be more familiar with guiding her. Eventually, it may be that sighted peers in the coaching session would be able to assist. Again a touching protocol needs to be established with the athlete.

It is the decision of the coach and the performer, whether or not it is safe or appropriate to be coached in those sports. For specific information on coaching performers with a visual impairment, you are recommended to contact British Blind Sport (address in Appendix E).

Performers who are deaf or hard of hearing

Communicating with hard of hearing or deaf performers may create even greater challenges. How would you need to adapt your communication skills to coach someone who is hard of hearing? In completing the next activity, remember deafness is a hearing loss which makes it impossible to understand speech through hearing alone, even if a hearing aid is used. Hearing aids may need to be removed depending on the nature of the activity. There is usually a need for another means of communication such as lip-reading or signing.

ACTIVITY 7

1   Read the profile of John Smith:

> *John Smith*[1]
> *John, aged 24, is a manual worker in an animal feeds factory. His favourite sport is football and he is a member of his local village side, being the leading goal scorer in the 1996/97 season. John attends circuit training sessions each week at a local leisure centre and in the football season attends club coaching sessions twice each week, with a match every Sunday. Out of the football season, John swims, plays tennis and occasionally goes jogging. Among his sporting ambitions, John lists a desire to play at Wembley. John has some residual hearing and wears a hearing aid.*

2   Imagine you are going to introduce John into one of your coaching sessions. Jot down how you would need to adapt your communication skills in order to work efficiently with him:

Now turn over.

1   Biographical details correct at time of publication.

As with all performers, it is beneficial to take time to get to know John to establish the most appropriate means of communication. As he has residual hearing and uses a hearing aid, it is possible to communicate with him orally. However, John will also need to see your mouth so he has the opportunity to lip-read. This will reinforce what you are saying. For more information on hearing impairments, see Appendix A. The sort of factors you may have listed include the following:

- *Ensure your face is well-lit. For example if out of doors, face the sun as this will assist John who may be lip-reading or reading signs.*

- *Face John at all times when speaking to him. If you turn your head, he will no longer be able to read your lips.*

- *Do not chew, shout or cover your mouth with your hand when talking – this will again prevent John lip-reading effectively.*

- *Remember lip-reading is not a precise way of communicating. Do not presume if John can lip-read, he will understand every word. Much of lip-reading is intelligent guesswork.*

- *Ensure the coaching or competition environment is accommodating (eg no background noise to interfere with John's concentration).*

- *You may need to be near John to attract his attention (eg by tapping on his shoulder). Other means of attracting his attention may need to be established such as flicking lights on and off or waving.*

- *Keep sentences simple and avoid unnecessary jargon. This is particularly important for John as he was born with a hearing loss and his language skills (written and spoken) will be based on different principles to those of standard English. It is always useful to establish the meaning of any sport-specific or technical language before you start a session.*

- *Check John has understood what has been said.*

- *Provide written information if relevant but do not give John the written information to read and then continue to speak – he will be unable to lip-read or even be aware you are speaking.*

- *Be aware that John may be able to read your lips even if you are standing a distance from him and not talking to him.*

You will subsequently be able to plan an individual programme with John. If John has to remove his hearing aid, for example in training and competition, it is useful to establish mutually identifiable signs or gestures before he removes the aid. This will also help other participants such as teammates. It is important to raise your voice when John is not wearing his hearing aid.

You may be approached by a deaf performer who, unlike John, is unable to communicate orally. Again, you will have to establish the most appropriate means of communication. This may mean:

- using an interpreter who might be a parent, friend or teacher or a fully qualified individual – the Royal National Institute for the Deaf (RNID) will be able to provide you with information regarding hiring professional interpreters (address in Appendix E)
- learning to sign or finger spell – RNID will again be able to advise
- establishing mutually identifiable signs or gestures
- identifying whether or not the performer can lip-read.

Deaf performers can achieve and require the same coaching expertise as hearing performers. However, it is useful to appreciate that many deaf people refer to themselves as *the deaf*. This can be associated with the fact that being deaf is a cultural issue as well as a description of an impairment group. Deaf culture can be difficult for hearing people to understand and accept, and can lead to misunderstandings and frustration.

Although deaf performers can compete and be coached in the same situation as hearing performers, they often prefer to be in situations with other deaf performers. This can be for a number of reasons, including cultural similarities and communication issues. As a coach, it is important to respect the performer's **choice** and appreciate the strong cultural identity of some deaf performers.

Communicating with other disabled performers

So far you have considered how to adapt your communication skills to suit the needs of performers with a visual or hearing impairment. Table 1 over the page gives you further useful pointers in communicating with performers with other disabilities. It is again important to emphasise these pointers are made in very general terms and the more familiar a coach becomes with a performer, the easier it will be to establish successful communication strategies. You may wish to refer back to this table in subsequent activities.

Table 1: Key pointers for successful communication

Wheelchair user	Address the performer, not the person who may accompany him/her. Talk to the performer face to face and at eye level. Either sit down or kneel but be in a comfortable position if you intend to hold a long conversation. Talk to the performer with the sun or light shining on your face to illuminate it. Establish the level of understanding of the performer by asking questions or asking for a demonstration. The last two points are, of course, important coaching points for all performers.
Performer with cerebral palsy	Individuals with cerebral palsy may have a speech impairment. This should not automatically be associated with the individual having a learning disability (although some individuals may have). Individual performers may have devised individual means to communicate. It is useful to spend time getting to know the performer in order to learn and understand these means of communication. Don't pretend you understand; don't finish sentences for the athlete.
Performer with a learning disability	Establish the extent instructions and directions are understood. It is useful to remember to use simple, brief, concise language, without being patronising. Refer to performers according to their chronological age and encourage other performers, officials and supporters to use appropriate age and sport-specific terminology (eg in athletics, 'you paced yourself well' rather than 'good boy'). Some people with learning disabilities may use a signing system to support speech called Makaton. The individuals are not necessarily deaf or have no speech, but may be unable to communicate effectively by oral methods alone. For more information on Makaton, contact the Makaton Vocabulary Development Project, 31 Firwood Drive, Camberley, Surrey GU15 3QD. Tel: 01276-681390, Fax: 01276-681368, Website: www.makaton.org, E-mail: mvdp@makaton.org

4.2 Planning and Organising Sessions and Programmes

Having established a few guidelines about safety and medical factors, and how to improve your ability to communicate effectively with disabled performers, next you need to consider **what** to coach. Are the session requirements any different? Do you need to adapt the content of your coaching sessions, as well as the way you communicate when coaching?

All the general principles of how to establish goals and plan and organise coaching sessions are equally applicable when coaching disabled performers[1]. In addition, you will need to think carefully about the following:

- Are additional safety checks and constraints necessary?

- The need for setting individual goals with athletes is important.

- How to adapt the way you deliver and organise the session to accommodate everyone.

- The length, intensity and frequency of sessions as well as the drills or activities within each session. For example, some disabled athletes tire more quickly, others need regular rests to avoid pressure sores, some have difficulty regulating temperature and need to rehydrate more frequently.

- The structure of the session. You may need to:
  - be creative in finding a variety of ways to explain or develop a particular skill
  - adapt drills and warm-ups to accommodate the needs of particular athletes
  - modify equipment and adapt rules to maximise opportunities for participation and ensure success.

Are the programme requirements any different?

- When planning a series of sessions over a period of time, perhaps leading to a competition, which factors need to be incorporated to achieve a balanced training programme?

- Consideration of physical, psychological, technical, tactical and lifestyle development needs of the athlete are needed.

- What long-term goals need to be agreed with the athlete?

- How can the appropriate sequencing of sessions and phased development of activities help the athlete to achieve their full potential?[2]

In addition to these general pointers, there are specific factors to consider when coaching people with different types of disability – some of these are shared in the following sections.

---

1 For further guidance, you are recommended to read Chapter Two of the **scUK** handbook *The Successful Coach*.

2 For further guidance, you are recommended to read the **scUK** guide to *Planning Coaching Programmes*.

Performers with physical disabilities

Inevitably there is more forward planning and organisation to consider when coaching performers with physical disabilities. To help you consider how to plan, organise and run coaching sessions for athletes with physical disabilities, you will first be introduced to two more performers – David and Anthony. You may also need to refer back to Activity 3 based on Tanni Grey's profile (page 12) and Table 1 on communication (page 36).

Dave McCrae[1]

David, aged 33, is the coordinator for Team Sport Scotland with responsibility for sport for disabled people. Dave's sport is standing volleyball and he was a member of the British Paralympic team in Atlanta. He holds coaching qualifications in football and volleyball. Dave's training schedule includes two team or squad training sessions each week, two aerobic style sessions such as running or cross training plus national league matches and disabled team squad sessions. Among his ambitions, he would like to win a Paralympic medal and play golf with Jack Nicklaus. Dave is a right below knee amputee and he wears a prosthesis.

Anthony Hughes[1]

Anthony, aged 37, is a tutor and head of department of Manufacturing Products and Textiles at the Derwen College in Shropshire. A former shot-put champion, his greatest achievements were obtaining a silver medal at the World Games in 1990 and retaining the British and European records until 1992. Anthony has now retired from competition and is focusing on developing a young athletics squad to elite level. One of his squad members, David Dudley, won a silver medal in the shot-put event at the Atlanta Paralympics. Anthony will be formalising his coaching this year by taking the Club Coach qualification. He intends to go on to train to be a Senior Coach and would like to be part of the British Paralympic Association's core staff for athletics. Anthony has Becker Muscular Dystrophy[2] and is a wheelchair user.

---

1   Biographical details correct at time of publication.

2   This is one of a number of conditions that affect the muscle fibres and cause muscle weakness.

Both David and Anthony are members of a disability sports organisation called the British Amputees Les Autres Sports Association (BALASA)[1]. Conditions which may result in a performer being classed as a Les Autres athlete include:

- amputation at or below the wrist or ankle

- arthrosis[2] of the major joints

- some types of cerebral palsy

- congenital conditions[3] affecting locomotion

- locomotor disabilities resulting in permanent disability resulting from fire, fractures, injuries to the musculoskeletal or nervous systems

- mutilated hands or feet

- head injuries that result in locomotor disorders

- multiple sclerosis – a condition where the messages to and from the brain are interrupted due to scarring on the spinal cord (for more information see Appendix A)

- muscular dystrophy – a hereditary condition causing progressive weakness and wasting of muscles (for more information see Appendix A).

For more information, contact BALASA (address in Appendix E).

Study the following session plans before trying Activity 8. Sessions A and B are sample volleyball coaching sessions for Dave. In Session A, Dave trains with non-disabled players. Session B is for disabled players only. Session C is a shot-put session for Anthony.

---

1   BALASA was formed from two original organisations – one for amputees and one for Les Autres. The Les Autres group refers to athletes who do not fit into any of the other NDSOs.

2   Arthrosis is a degenerative, non-inflammatory disease of the joints.

3   Congenital refers to conditions present or occurring at the time of birth but not necessarily hereditary.

Session Planner A	

Date: 28 August 1997	Venue: Kilmarnock Volleyball Club
Time: 7pm	Duration: 1.5 hours
Group/Performers: Kilmarnock Men's 1st & 2nd teams. GB Paralympic standing volleyball team member in session	Number in Session: 16
	Equipment Required:

Goals of Session: To improve field defence technique

Time	Organisation/Presentation	Coaching Points
15 mins	**Warm-up/Introduction** Raise body temperature – running (10 mins) and associated movements. Light, gentle mobility exercises followed by drill with partner. Stretch after the drill.	
65 mins	**Main Content** • Defensive technique drill: Feeder to unit of three (rotate). • Defensive tactical drill: Attacker to positions 1, 6 and 5. Blocker is added after ten feeds. • Conditioned game: Units of three (1, 6, 5). One blocker mid net, first to five points then off. • Full game.	All movement made prior to contact. Fixed feet, head forward, relaxed from shoulder to wrist. Parallel lines head/shoulder/hips/knees. ADDITIONAL POINTS FOR BELOW KNEE AMPUTEE: Reaffirm fix body as opponent contacts. Spread weight bearing to prosthesis (no weak side!). Fix hips into mid court target area. Don't allow core area to collapse on impaired side. Soft/relaxed contact upper arms.
10 mins	**Cool-down/Summary** Light jog and stretch.	

Injuries	Evaluation/Action

Session Planner B	

Date: 19 July 1997	**Venue:** Manchester Metropolitan University
Time: 10am	**Duration:** 2.5 hours
Group/Performers: GB disabled standing volleyball team (paralympic)	**Number in Session:** 12
	Equipment Required:

Goals of Session: To improve attack technique and efficiency

Time	Organisation/Presentation	Coaching Points
15 mins	**Warm-up/Introduction** Running to raise body temperature; upper limb impairments — round full court, double lower limb and single above knee impairments — cross court, single lower limb impairments — discretional. Mobility: Easy, gentle limb stretches through progressive range of movement — balanced mobility exercises through impaired areas.	Encourage gentle to vigorous mobile and ballistic shoulder and arm movements (progressive).
125 mins	**Main Content** ROTATIONAL DRILL — SETTER SPECIALIST: Easy feed to passer, pass to setter, set to attacker, attack! All players begin approach around 3m attack line (less for greater lower limb impairments). Weight forwards, slide lead foot, step and release dual footed jump. Draw body upwards from centre line (sternum). Arm impairments, take both sides up powerfully (emphasis on impaired side). Encourage power from core body area. Reinforce technical information. Specialising information to individual impairments. Emphasise rhythm to all players regardless of impairment, release approach on setters touch. PROGRESSION: Add extra passer; add zone 3 or zone 2 attacker; extend feed; full service feed; attack feed from gymnastic box. PRESSURE CANNON DRILL: Rotational drill — pressure drill on attacker, must beat 3 defenders from pass & set. 1-point kill, 0-point defended, 2-points deducted direct error. Upper limb impaired 8+ and leave drill, single below knee 7+ and leave drill, single above knee 5+ and leave drill and double lower leg 1+ and leave drill.	All players begin approach around 3m attack line (less for greater lower limb impairments). Weight forwards, slide lead foot, step and release dual footed jump. Draw body upwards from centre line (sternum). Arm impairments, take both sides up powerfully (emphasis on impaired side). Encourage power from core body area. Reinforce technical information. Specialising information to individual impairments. Emphasise rhythm to all players regardless of impairment, release approach on setters touch.
10 mins	**Cool-down/Summary** Light running, quick walking — relevant to impairment. Easy movement through full range of all upper limb movements. Easy mobility through all limb movements.	

Injuries	Evaluation/Action

Session Planner C		
Date: 16 April 1998		**Venue:** Derwen College, Gobowen
Time: 5pm		**Duration:** 3 hours
Group/Performers: Anthony Hughes		**Number in Session:** 1
		Equipment Required:

Goals of Session: Develop speed and endurance using good technique

Time	Organisation/Presentation	Coaching Points
30 mins	**Warm-up/Introduction** Stretching and mobility exercises. Using 1kg shot, throw five sets of five. Using 3kg shot, throw three warm-up throws.	
120 mins	**Main Content** Throw 3kg shot for distance x10. Rest 30 mins. Throw 3kg shots for distance x5. Consider the time taken to transfer from wheelchair to throwing frame and back again.	Concentrate on good technique/distance — aim for 5—7 good throws out of ten.
30 mins	**Cool-down/Summary** Using 1kg shot, three throws. Stretch and mobility.	Consider the time taken to change, shower etc.
Injuries	**Evaluation/Action**	

ACTIVITY 8

Consider how would you need to adapt the content of your coaching sessions to meet the needs of Dave and/or Anthony. It may be useful to bear in mind the following prompts:

- Dave and Anthony's long- and short-term goals.
- Their experience of sport and your sport in particular.
- The type of activity.
- The type of sport.
- The organisation required (inclusion, integration).
- Warm-ups.

Dave:

Anthony:

Now turn over.

Dave

When working with Dave in your sport, you would have to consider the following:

- *How movement is affected.*
- *What movement patterns are already established.*
- *Any poor technique that may need to be re-taught.*
- *His level of motivation and personal goals.*
- *Dave's understanding of personal safety and medical care.*
- *Whether or not Dave could be fully integrated into the session.*
- *The nature of your sport – is it feasible to participate? Is it a contact sport or is there danger of damage to the prosthesis? Is it a team sport? This might affect the extent to which Dave could be integrated.*
- *An appropriate warm-up, for example the one from Session Plan B on page 41.*

If you were approached by an amputee performer other than Dave, there are certain additional factors you would need to take into consideration:

- *It is helpful to realise that Dave was born an amputee – some performers may have had a leg amputated as a result of accident or disease so may cope with their impairment in a different way.*
- *The age of the performer.*
- *Which limb or part of limb is missing?*
- *Does the performer use a wheelchair?*
- *Does the performer need any assistance?*
- *Is the amputation acquired or congenital? This may affect, for example, the length of time a performer may be able to train as some congenital amputees have less stump soreness than amputees who have lost a limb through injury.*
- *Has the performer had time to adjust to the loss of a limb? Frustration at being unable to do something may lead to outbursts of anger.*
- *Are specific exercises needed to strengthen the remaining muscles in for example above knee amputees, to ensure muscle wastage does not occur?*
- *Phantom pain or other sensations may appear to occur in the amputated portion of the limb. This may cause discomfort or embarrassment to performers who may be reluctant at first to tell coaches.*

Amputee performers are able to participate in most sports, although the type of amputation will influence the choice of sport. For example, it may be difficult for an arm amputee to pole-vault as both arms are needed to perform the vault. However, there would probably be little or no difficulty in competing in running events and training could be the same as that of a non-disabled athlete. Dave trains with and coaches a non-disabled volleyball team which competes in the Scottish national league and also at international level for the British Disabled Volleyball Team for standing volleyball. If Dave, or any other amputee, required further assistance on personal safety, prosthesis and medical care, they should be directed to the British Amputees Les Autres Sports Association (BALASA), address in Appendix E.

Anthony

When working with Anthony, you may have considered some of the following points:

- *Are venues for competition and coaching accessible?*

- *Anthony may need additional consideration because of the medical and safety requirements of his condition, in particular in relation to:*
  - *fatigue*
  - *day-to-day variations in ability that could affect such things as balance and swollen joints*
  - *pressure damage*
  - *cardiovascular performance*
  - *mobility and the logistics of getting to the venue (eg physical effort in moving self and equipment)*
  - *transfers, for example from a wheelchair to a throwing frame[1].*

If coaching Les Autres performers, you will also need to consider advice related to their specific condition.

Wheelchair performers

The term wheelchair athletes refers to all spinal paralysed persons and persons with equated disorders, who require a wheelchair to compete in relevant sports, or as specified in the rules of the sports section (International Stoke Mandeville Wheelchair Sports Federation (ISMWSF) 1989). Generally, this means that in order for performers to be eligible to compete in wheelchair events, they must have at least a 10% loss of function in their lower limbs. Some of the more usual conditions which may result in individuals being eligible to compete as wheelchair athletes include:

- traumatic paraplegia and tetraplegia (ie spinal cord injuries)
- spina bifida
- post poliomyelitis impairment[2]
- limb amputation
- cerebral palsy
- other non-ambulant athlete (see page 39).

---

1   Throwing frames are specially made structures to support a performer in a throwing event.

2   Poliomyelitis is a virus infection which attacks the spinal cord and causes paralysis.

You have already met Tanni (page 12) who is a wheelchair athlete. Now read the profile about Di who has paraplegia and is also a wheelchair athlete.

> *Diana Bowles*[1]
> *Di, aged 39, is a retired nurse and lives in Cheshire. Di's main sport is wheelchair tennis and in the last few years, she has made a steady climb in the British rankings. Di has achieved success in both singles and doubles tournaments with her partner Chris Smith, at home and abroad. Her schedule includes individual coaching for one hour each week, team coaching for three hours each week plus additional match practice for three hours each week. Di's other interests include swimming for two hours each week and taking her dog, Solo, for a walk each day. Her aspirations for the future include accumulating enough ranking points to enable her to compete in the open division of wheelchair tennis. Di has paraplegia.*

1   Biographical details correct at time of publication.

ACTIVITY 9

Consider how you might need to plan, organise and run a coaching session for a wheelchair athlete. Could Diana be integrated into your coaching session? Would you need to adapt the session? Would you run a separate session? What would you need to consider prior to and during the session?

Now turn over.

You may or may not have been able to accommodate Di within your usual coaching session. You will probably have readily considered all the issues related to transport, access (into and within the venue – for example, can she negotiate steps?) but did you also consider the following:

- *Whether Di requires assistance (for example, when getting into a swimming pool, having refreshments) and if so, how would this be provided.*

- *How to respect Di's independence and space around her chair. For example, it is generally accepted that you should not:*
  - *move Di when seated in her wheelchair – ask her to move*
  - *lean on her wheelchair or hang things from it*
  - *assume she needs a push or additional help, for example, when carrying a kit bag – always ask*

- *How you might need to adapt the way you coach the skills, organise the activities or adapt the rules or equipment to make the session enjoyable and worthwhile for both disabled and non-disabled athletes.*

More guidance is offered in the feedback following Activity 10 (page 56). It may also help to look at the following session plans for wheelchair athletes. Session D is a track session for a group of wheelchair users. Session E includes a wheelchair athlete with the use of upper body only within a swimming training session.

Session Planner D	
Date: 2 August 1997	**Venue:** Alexandra Stadium
Time: 10am	**Duration:** 2 hours
Group/Performers: Junior squad	**Number in Session:** 8
	Equipment Required:

Goals of Session: To improve speed endurance

Time	Organisation/Presentation	Coaching Points
30 mins	**Warm-up/Introduction** 3–4 steady laps (10 mins). General stretch (5 mins). 2 steady laps (5 mins). Full stretch (10 mins).	
70 mins	**Main Content** 6 starts (full command, pick up speed fast, good hand speed. Push 30–35 metres). Pyramid 100m, 200m, 300m, 400m, 500m up and down, 300m rolling in between. Consider lane use by wheelchair users and able-bodied athletes.	Watch for good technique throughout session. Concentrate on lifting arms.
20 mins	**Cool-down/Summary** 4–5 laps and stretch	
Injuries	**Evaluation/Action**	

Session Planner E		

Date: 30 November 1997	**Venue:** Fife Sports Stadium
Time: 4.30pm	**Duration:** 1 hour
Group/Performers: Scottish squad	**Number in Session:** Approx 20
	Equipment Required:

Goals of Session: Endurance training session

Time	Organisation/Presentation	Coaching Points
7 mins	**Warm-up/Introduction** Continuous swim — change stroke every second length (no butterfly). Think long, stretched and relaxed. 250m	Think long, stretched and relaxed.
40 mins	**Main Content** DRILLS: 4x50m (first length drill, second length full stroke). 30 seconds rest. First and second strokes. 200m	Wheelchair athletes use drills (for example, drills for upper body: use clenched fists, two strokes with the left arm then two with the right, single arm slow strokes) that are suited to their functional ability and use their competition stroke instead of the full stroke.
	MAIN SET: 4x100m full stroke. 45 seconds rest. First and second strokes. 400m	Concentrate on turns, keep tight and tidy.
	CONTRAST: 3x75m individual medley. 30 seconds rest. 225m	
	Tumble turn on freestyle and backstroke if possible.	Wheelchair athletes use a turn which is most suited to their functional ability and which is as quick as possible.
	Spend the final ten minutes practising starts and turns.	
7 mins	**Cool-down/Summary** 100–200m swim-down	
Injuries	**Evaluation/Action**	

In order to establish the functional ability of a performer who is a wheelchair user, it is best to **ask the individual** and **never** assume anything. Coaches often assume the ability of a performer in accordance with stereotyped images gained from what they have read or what they have been told about certain conditions. The message is still the same – treat the performer as an individual and focus on what he/she **can** do, not what he/she **cannot** do.

Performers with a learning disability

When working with performers with a learning disability, coaches may need to make significant adaptations to content, dependent on the individual. You will always need to:

- be patient, tolerant, consistent and tactful but ensure performers understand the boundaries of acceptable behaviour

- make sessions fun and enjoyable (this of course should always be the aim)

- break down complex skills into simpler steps but ensure you link them together

- be aware that the motor skills and physical fitness of some performers may be generally poor due to lack of opportunities to participate in sporting activities or even regular day-to-day exercise

- enable simple decision-making

- avoid drills that rely heavily on numeracy and literacy skills

- teach by showing and copying, not telling.

- be aware of a high incidence of epilepsy.

It is useful to remember that the cause of a performer's learning disability may also affect an individual's development physically, socially and emotionally as well as intellectually. You are advised to seek help and guidance before coaching an athlete with learning disabilities.

Performers with Down's syndrome

People with Down's syndrome can have varying degrees of learning disability. It may be useful to look at employment and level of independence to appreciate the many differences in ability of people with Down's syndrome. For example, some can hold full-time jobs, others work in sheltered workshops, while some cannot work. Similarly, some people can live fully independent lives while others live in supported settings, with the degree of support depending on their abilities. Read about Sally-Anne.

> *Sally-Anne Bourne[1]*
> *Sally-Anne, aged 30, is an administrative clerk with HTV (Harlech Television) in Cardiff. Her main sport is swimming and she has won many medals at home and internationally. Sally-Anne trains with a swimming club for people with special needs and also with Cardiff Masters Swimming Club, where she concentrates on stamina training. She also enjoys athletics, basketball and badminton. Sally-Anne's main hope for the future is to be selected to compete at a Paralympic Games. She has Down's syndrome.*

1   Biographical details correct at time of publication.

If you were to coach Sally-Anne, you first need to establish:

- her physical ability and skill level

- her ability to learn sport-specific rules

- her individual strengths and challenges. You need to set her challenging and realistic goals and encourage her to meet the requirements of the sport in practice sessions rather than making allowances.

Next it may help to know a little more about possible personal safety and medical requirements of performers with Down's syndrome. For example, some may have a condition called Atlanto-axial instability[1]. It is useful to remember that Down's syndrome is not a medical condition and does not in itself have medical implications. However, people with Down's syndrome are susceptible to chest infections and colds. About a quarter of babies born have a heart defect (usually a hole in the heart or defective valve) which can usually be corrected by surgery.

As in all coaching, performers with Down's syndrome should be accepted and assessed as individuals with individual strengths and challenges.

Performers with cerebral palsy

You have already met Dean who has cerebral palsy (page 24). It is important to remember that as a performer with cerebral palsy, Dean's needs will be totally different from any other performer with the same condition. Dean is able to take charge of his own personal safety and medical needs but sometimes requires additional support because of his physical disability. Sport has specific benefits for Dean – improving muscle control, flexibility, posture, balance and coordination and cardiorespiratory efficiency, especially breathing. To plan a training programme efficiently and effectively, you will need to take the time to build an understanding relationship with Dean.

It is helpful to be aware that performers with cerebral palsy may be more likely to have epilepsy than their non-disabled peers. If a performer has epilepsy, it is useful to establish how he/she copes with seizures on a personal basis and what procedures you should follow (see Appendix C). Some performers may have a degree of learning disability as well as a physical disability plus other associated considerations such as a speech impediment.

---

1   Atlanto-axial instability is a slackness of the ligaments which hold the joints stable in the neck. For more information see Appendix A.

When organising training sessions or attendance at events for performers with cerebral palsy, it is necessary to take the following into consideration:

- Is transport required? If so, does the transport need to be wheelchair accessible (not all performers are ambulant – able to walk).

- Is the venue accessible? This will include social areas and changing areas as well as parking, coaching and competition areas.

- Is the overnight accommodation accessible? If the performer uses a battery powered wheelchair, are there facilities to recharge?

- If the performer requires assistance to attend coaching sessions, is there an enabler (relative or friend) available who can support the performer? Is the enabler fully aware of what is and is not required when supporting the performer? As a coach, you may need to establish boundaries regarding responsibilities – for example the performer's personal needs and how to assist during a coaching session if required.

- What special equipment do you need? Information can be obtained from Cerebral Palsy Sport (Address in Appendix E). Throwing frames will need to be tied down. Are there areas to do this?

- What level of support do you require? Consideration needs to be given to:
  - personal requirements, dressing, using the toilet, eating
  - transport
  - help with training programmes – establish who does what. Do you need any specific safety or medical consideration (see Appendix A)?
  - what levels of awareness do the facility staff have? What training have they undertaken?

4.3 Planning Your Sessions

You have now been offered some principles about planning, organising and running a coaching session for performers with a range of disabilities. This will give you some general guidelines, which combined with your existing coaching experience, will stand you in good stead when starting to plan your own session. However, always be wary of making assumptions – every performer is different even if he/she seems to have similar disabilities. In addition, you will need to roll up your sleeves and start to coach disabled performers before you can really begin to plan and run effective sessions. Wherever possible, seek guidance from other coaches who have knowledge and experience of coaching disabled athletes. Nevertheless, start to put into practice the information you have gained in this pack by trying the next activity.

ACTIVITY 10

Having read about the need for good planning and organisation when coaching disabled performers, in this activity you are asked to identify the key issues you would need to consider when planning a coaching session for one of each of the following:

1 Sally-Anne, Di or Dean.

2 Another disabled performer you know.

3 One other performer you have met through this pack (eg Tanni, Dave, Anthony, John, Marsha).

In addition to your usual session planning skills, you will need to consider things such as:

• transport and access to the venues – where you coach, other competition venues

• the requirements of your sport (eg equipment, clothing)

• the type of sport (eg team/individual, indoor/outdoor, contact/non-contact)

• additional safety factors

• communication issues

• the length of the session

• specific issues relating to the particular disability.

To help you, go back and read the relevant sections about the particular disability in the pack and the relevant appendix, also draw on your own coaching experience:

Name of Performer 1:

Key points:

Name of Performer 2:

Key points:

Name of Performer 3:

Key points:

Now turn over.

In practice, the first thing you should do is talk to the individual performer to establish what he/she wants from a coaching session – this should be no different from your current practice with all other performers. Information on competition opportunities and rule changes can be obtained from the NDSO or the NGB (addresses in Appendix E). Compare your points with the following issues considered for Sally-Anne, Di and Dean – you will have probably noted similar issues for each performer:

Physical access

Sally-Anne should have few or no problems with physical access to facilities. However, both Di and Dean would need wheelchair access to all areas. Di uses a manual wheelchair and the nature of her disabling condition and level of personal fitness means she is able to negotiate small single steps. However, Dean uses a battery operated wheelchair which is very heavy and may not be able to negotiate steps of any kind. Once again, communicating with the performers will give you a clear picture of their needs to ensure access.

Transport

You may have to take transport into consideration when planning a session or competition. Di is able to drive herself to coaching sessions but Dean and Sally-Anne would require transport of a different nature. Dean would either need wheelchair accessible public transport or an enabler to drive him to sessions. Sally-Anne would be able to use public transport, always assuming coaching sessions are timed to coincide with bus or train timetables and issues such as women travelling alone at night, are considered.

Equipment

You may have to advise some performers of appropriate equipment – for example, which is the most suitable footwear for certain events or what kind of clothing to wear in certain weather conditions. Specialist equipment such as sports wheelchairs, throwing frames and so on may be needed. For example, if Di were to take part in a field event such as discus throwing, she may need a specially designed throwing frame which can be transported to venues and fixed to the ground. Di could then transfer from her wheelchair to the frame to throw. Advice on suitable equipment can be obtained from the appropriate NDSO, (addresses in Appendix E) or from the relevant NGB. In some instances, minor adjustments to equipment may be required. For example, using a lighter racket or a more brightly coloured ball.

Coaching time

You may have decided it would be more beneficial to coach performers on an individual basis for all or part of a session. It may be useful to refer back to the Winnick Model (page 10) to see the various choices available for coaches and performers. For example, in a tennis coaching session, Sally-Anne and Di could attend warm-up sessions alongside able-bodied players. Some skill training sessions could be shared but Di may need more practice on wheelchair manoeuvrability. Tactical and technique sessions could be shared, with individual assistance being given where required to all performers, not just those with a disability. Small and large game sessions could also be shared according to the abilities of individual players. It is for competition purposes that performers may choose to be segregated and compete within their own disability groups. Dean could join in but may need one-to-one assistance. In team games such as basketball, performers could be integrated for most parts of a coaching session (basketball can be played by people with different impairments in the same team) but again may prefer competition within a disability group setting.

Safety/Injury Prevention

The normal safety requirements of your sport would apply but you may also need to take some of the following points into consideration:

- *Performers with a hearing impairment may not be able to hear verbal warnings.*

- *Performers with a visual impairment, although able to hear a warning, may be unsure which way to go if they are unable to see.*

It is essential to establish safety procedures, for example in the event of fire, at the beginning of any coaching or competition situation to avoid any confusion. Sometimes performers are unaware of danger in certain situations and may need to be either constantly reminded of the danger or be asked to move from the situation. Sally-Anne, Di and Dean are all aware of the safety precautions they have to consider for themselves. For example, Sally-Anne, being fair skinned, is aware of the effects of too much sun, Di is aware that she needs to change her seating position occasionally to avoid pressure sores and Dean is aware that occasionally if he goes into spasm, he could knock his legs or arms against a table. Performers should be encouraged to look after their own well-being. Further advice can be obtained from the disability sports organisations (addresses in Appendix E).

It is impossible to answer all the questions you may have in this pack. It is recommended you either contact your own sports governing body or the appropriate disability sports organisation, or an experienced coach you know who may be able to help. You are also recommended to attend the **scUK** taught workshop. Talking to the performer and fully understanding his/her needs will give you additional confidence and an insight into how to adapt your coaching practice to meet each performer's requirements.

4.4 Designing and Running Programmes and Sessions

Using your own coaching experience, the pointers identified in the previous activity together with the preceding sample session plans (pages 40–42, 49–50) and the following plan (page 58), you should now feel ready to try planning a session for a disabled performer in your sport. First study all the examples, then try Activity 11.

Session F is a wheelchair tennis session.

	Session Planner F	
Date: 14 July 1997		**Venue:** Wrexham ITT
Time: 1.30pm		**Duration:** 1 hour
Group/Performers: Experienced players		**Number in Session:** 4
		Equipment Required:

Goals for Session: Continued improvement of forehand technique

Time	Organisation/Presentation	Coaching Points
15 mins	**Warm-up/Introduction** Slow push around court, arm stretches, hitting across net in service boxes — moving to baseline as become warmer, rallying in half courts — forehands only.	
30 mins	**Main Content** Play half court singles — 11 points. Look for correct techniques under pressure. Move to doubles — see how players continue techniques consistently under more pressure. Watch players hit — concentrate on forehand.	LOOK FOR: • reading the ball • movement to ball • positioning of wheelchair • execution of stroke.
15 mins	**Cool-down/Summary** Hitting from baseline, move into net and tap over net. Stretches. Slow push around court.	
Injuries	**Evaluation/Action**	

ACTIVITY II

Select a performer to coach in your sport – this may be an actual person you know or one of the disabled athletes to whom you have been introduced in this pack. Using the general guidelines and information offered in this pack, devise two coaching sessions for the named individual:

- who you have agreed to include in your next club coaching session – show how you would adapt your session to integrate the new member

- and a group of his/her disabled friends who have been meeting informally to have fun participating in your sport and have expressed an interest in having some coaching – show how you would devise a session to meet the needs of the group.

For each situation, you will need to consider all the relevant pointers in the previous activity plus more specific issues such as how to:

- identify the session goals and devise appropriate content to achieve them

- structure and organise the session – to meet every performer's goals

- build in some flexibility to help you adapt the session as necessary once you have a better idea of the abilities of the performer/s

- develop skills – there may be a need to adapt the actual technique or perhaps how you teach it

- maximise enjoyment and success – consider the time spent on drills, how competition can be managed and how some feelings of achievement can be assured.

Continued...

Session Planner	
Date:	Venue:
Time:	Duration:
Group/Performers:	Number in Session:
	Equipment Required:

Goals of Session:

Time	Organisation/Presentation	Coaching Points
	Warm-up/Introduction	
	Main Content	
	Cool-down/Summary	

Additional Considerations (Transport, Accessibility)

Session Planner	
Date:	Venue:
Time:	Duration:
Group/Performers:	Number in Session:
	Equipment Required:

Goals of Session:

Time	Organisation/Presentation	Coaching Points
	Warm-up/Introduction	
	Main Content	
	Cool-down/Summary	

Additional Considerations (Transport, Accessibility)

You may have found this quite difficult – particularly if you selected a performer you had never met before and were unfamiliar with his/her goals and needs. This hypothetical situation is inevitably artificial but it will have forced you to try to adapt your coaching practice in the light of the information you have gained by working through this pack. If you were able to use a disabled athlete you already know, have perhaps watched or even started to coach, the exercise will have been much more realistic. Equally if you are going to (or have already) attended the workshop, you will gain some actual hands-on experience from which you can draw guidance.

Whatever the situation, the most important thing to check the effectiveness of your plan, is to try running the session and monitoring carefully exactly what happened. What went well, what did not go well and may need to be adapted in the future? Remember you will not become an expert overnight – you will need to develop your skills and experience. This will only happen as you start to coach disabled performers and more rapidly if you can either observe a more experienced coach work or use that coach as a sounding board to test out your ideas and help meet the challenges as they arise[1].

4.5 Recap and Action Plan

You may now feel ready to take the next step. You may have gained new knowledge and perhaps confidence to help with the coaching you are already doing with disabled athletes. You may feel very excited and ready to accept the challenge of starting to coach – you may already know someone who is seeking coaching or you may wish to make contact with national or local disability groups to see how you could become involved. However, you may feel you have neither the confidence or perhaps desire to coach disabled performers – you may wish to go no further or perhaps become involved in helping other coaches from time to time.

Perhaps you are still unsure. Whatever you feel is the next step for you, you may wish to try one or more of the recommended action plans.

---

1 At the workshop, you will be helped to identify a possible mentor in your area to provide some ongoing help and support.

ACTION PLAN A

1 Find a coach[1] who is working with disabled athletes in your local area, in your sport or with the particular group of disabled athletes you would like to coach.

2 Arrange to meet with the coach before the session and find out as much as you can:

- How long has the coach been involved in coaching disabled performers and how did he/she get started?

- How long has the coach been working with the particular athlete/s?

- What are the goals and needs of the athlete/s?

- What are the main challenges the coach has had to overcome?

- What are the particular goals of the session you will watch? A copy of the session plan would be ideal if there is one available.

3 Observe the session and make detailed notes:

4 After the session, you may wish to spend some further time with the coach to seek answers to some of the questions you may have about the session, his/her approach, the participants or the way forward.

---

1 You will have been given some help to do this if you have already attended the workshop; if not, use the address list in Appendix E to help you.

ACTION PLAN B

If possible, you are strongly encouraged to try to run the session you designed in Activity 11 and complete a very detailed evaluation of what went well, what perhaps did not work as well as you might have expected, what you might do differently next time and what further information or help you might need. Remember if possible to try to spend some time with the participant/s to establish his/her goals and needs before you run the session – you may wish to modify some parts of the session planned. Record your evaluations and design the next coaching session based on your experiences.

Evaluations:

Session Planner		
Date:	Venue:	
Time:	Duration:	
Group/Performers:	Number in Session:	
	Equipment Required:	

Goals of Session:

Time	Organisation/Presentation	Coaching Points
	Warm-up/Introduction	
	Main Content	
	Cool-down/Summary	

Additional Considerations (Transport, Accessibility)

Notes

Competition

5.0 What's in It for You?

Some disabled participants may wish to compete. Therefore you need some background knowledge of the opportunities available for competition at local, regional and national levels, so you can advise and direct performers appropriately. In this chapter you will be introduced to the classification systems used in disability sport (further details in Appendix C) and by the end, you should be able to:

- explain why classification systems are necessary
- know where to find more detailed information.

Opportunities for competition are easier in some sports and with some disability groups than others. For example in athletics and swimming, there are competition opportunities for all disability groups. However, in some sports, you may find fewer opportunities – for example, an archer with cerebral palsy may find there is no competition against other people with a similar disability in that particular sport[1].

5.1 Classification Systems

Classification systems are designed to ensure fair and enjoyable competitions exist in non-disabled sport as well as disability sport. Stop to think what these are and why they are used.

---

1   In the UK there are more opportunities for people with cerebral palsy to compete in boccia, swimming, athletics and bowls than other sports.

ACTIVITY 12

1 Jot down ways in which sport uses some form of classification system (an example is given to get you started):

   • Segregation by sex

2 Mark the ones used in your sport with a tick.

3 Explain why the classifications are needed in your sport and comment on their effectiveness:

Now turn over.

1/2   You may have listed some of the following (and perhaps others):

- *Separation by age – for example, age group competitions occur in most sports; veterans' events are used in athletics and swimming meetings.*

- *Separation according to weight (for example in boxing and rowing or in AM league basketball, rugby league in Australia age group).*

- *Separation according to ability – for example, golf handicaps or table tennis leagues.*

3   To ensure safe and enjoyable competition. Frequent competition in which there is no possibility of winning is rarely enjoyable.

Classification systems have been developed by most of the major disability groups in order to hold even and fair competitions. The classification systems are recognised nationally and internationally. All disabled performers need a classification card that must be produced at every competition to ensure they are competing against performers of similar ability. Individuals are trained as classifiers and are then qualified to assess disabled performers to give them their classification card.

The following example of a classification card was kindly provided by the British Wheelchair Sports Foundation.

5.2 Advising a Performer

Classification has always been based on disability and the level of physical or mental impairment, with each disability sports organisation having its own classification system. However, there is a move towards a functional classification system. According to the 1996 Atlanta Paralympic Games General and Functional Classification Guide, this is the streamlining of the systems by combining classes with similar disabilities against performance levels. This means that people with different disabilities can compete together, being classified according to their level of performance and functional ability.

Classification systems can be complex and at times difficult to understand. Competition at different levels locally and nationally can often have different methods of classification. However, competition entry forms will always state the method of classification to be followed.

Different sports also have different methods of classifying competitors. For example, wheelchair tennis players compete against other players, beginning in the novice class, regardless of the type of impairment[1]. The players aim to win enough matches to enable them to move up the ranking system through c, b and a classes until they reach open class. It is always advisable to contact the appropriate national disability sports organisation for the most up-to-date advice on classification and competition opportunities.

ACTIVITY 13

1 For this activity you need either to:

- select one of the performers described in this pack or
- work with a disabled performer you know (this is the preferred option whenever possible).

2 Ask the performer (or reread the profile) to find out:

- the competition opportunities at local, regional, national and international levels:

- where the performer can obtain a classification card:

- where advice can be obtained about specialist equipment:

Now turn over.

---

1   Players with tetraplegia have their own competition structure.

If you had difficulty in finding some of the information, you may find Table 2 useful.

Table 2: Contacts

Information on	Where to Find it
International competition	*British Paralympic Association (BPA) for Paralympic sports only* *National Disability Sport Organisation (NDSO)* *National Governing Body of Sport (NGB)*
National competition	*NDSO* *NGB*
Regional/local competition	*NDSO* *NGB* *Home countries disability sports organisations*
Local competition (and clubs)	*NDSO* *NGB* *Local authority sports and leisure departments, local libraries*
Classification cards	*NDSO* *NGB*
Equipment	*NDSO* *NGB* *Home countries disability sports organisations*
Further information	*English Federation of Disability Sport (EFDS)* *Disability Sport Cymru* *Scottish Disability Sport* *Disability Sport NI*

Contact addresses and telephone numbers can be found in Appendix E.

If you were coaching Dave McCrae, for example, you could take the following route. Remember, Dave plays volleyball, lives in Scotland and is an amputee.

International Competition	– *BPA (sitting volleyball is a Paralympic sport)*
	– *British Amputees and Les Autres Sports Association (BALASA)*
	– *British Volleyball Federation (BVF)*
	– *Scottish Volleyball Association (SVA)*
National Competition	– *BALASA*
	– *BVF*
	– *SVA*
Regional/Local Competition	– *SVA*
	– *Scottish Disability Sport*
	– *sportscotland*
Local Competition	– *Edinburgh Council Sports Department*
	– *SVA*
Classification Card	– *BALASA*
Equipment – for example advice about prosthesis	– *BALASA*

5.3   Recap and Action Plan

This chapter has provided some guidance about who to contact for specific competition information relating to individual disabled performers – you will find some disability groups and sports easier to locate than others. All the organisations listed should be able to support and advise the performer and you the coach.

In this, and previous chapters, you have looked at the various ways you can adapt your coaching for a disabled performer and how you and the performer can identify appropriate sports opportunities and competition. The recommended action will give you some real insight into competitive sport for disabled athletes.

ACTION PLAN

Identify a competition held for disabled athletes – this may be local or if you have difficulty there are a number of regional and national events you might select, for example the Manchester Youth Games. If possible, find out the organiser and make contact to see if you could help in any way. If that is not possible, go as a spectator. Make a note of your observations and draw up a checklist to help you plan and enter a competitive event with one of your own disabled athletes in the future.

You may have considered:

- *location*
- *accommodation*
- *accessibility*
- *equipment requirements*
- *helpers/guides*
- *officials*
- *administrators*
- *medical assistance/attendance*
- *advertising*
- *programmes*
- *sponsorship*
- *records*
- *media contacts*
- *photography*
- *official guests.*

Conclusion

This pack cannot provide all the answers to every query about coaching disabled performers. However, it should have given you a sound foundation of advice, knowledge and skills and some direction to additional sources of information through the appendices.

By working through this study pack and completing the activities, you should have gained sufficient information to enable you to work confidently with disabled performers and adapt your coaching skills accordingly. Of course, your confidence will increase as you gain more experience. Attendance at the accompanying workshop will help to reinforce some of the key pointers in this pack, provide additional information, answer particular queries and concerns. Where the workshops are run for a specific sport, there will be an opportunity for hands on practical coaching experience. At the workshop, all coaches will be given advice about a possible mentor coach who could offer advice and support for you as you develop your coaching skills in this specialist area.

Notes

Further Information on Specific Disabilities

Cerebral palsy

Cerebral palsy is not a disease or illness. It is a brain lesion which is non-progressive and causes variable impairment of the coordination, tone and strength of muscle action impacting on postures and movement. The degree of impairment between individuals with cerebral palsy varies considerably according to the severity and site of the brain damage. No two people with cerebral palsy are alike because the brain damage which causes the condition can evolve differently in each individual. Every performer with cerebral palsy will therefore be different and coaches will need to bear this in mind. Nevertheless, the following points should also be considered. Cerebral palsy:

- is non-fatal, non-contagious, non-progressive but incurable
- has various symptoms according to the location and amount of brain damage
- has a range of symptoms from severe (total inability to control movements) to very mild (some people may have a slight speech impediment)
- is a condition where some individuals may have:
  - difficulty in coordinating and integrating basic movement patterns
  - associated conditions such as visual impairment, hearing impairment, learning disability, epilepsy, speech and language disorders, poor hand-eye control and coordination or a combination of all these.

Sport can improve cardiovascular function. Coaches who require more information on cerebral palsy are recommended to contact C P Sport (address in Appendix E) or their SCOPE regional office and Scottish equivalent.

Down's syndrome and atlanto-axial instability

In people with down's syndrome, the ligaments which normally hold the joints stable can be very slack. People with down's syndrome may therefore experience a greater range of movement of some joints than the population in general. One of the joints of the neck, the atlanto-axial joint, can be affected. As a result of this and because the actual bones of the joint may be poorly developed, people with down's syndrome could be more likely to experience a dislocation of the neck. Some research has shown that people who do not have down's syndrome may also be affected.

It is useful for coaches to be aware of early signs that a problem may be developing. Look out for:

- pain at a spot near the hard bump behind the ear
- a stiff neck which does not get better quickly
- alteration in the way a person walks so he/she appears less stable on his/her feet
- deterioration in a person's ability to manipulate things with his/her hands
- incontinence developing in a person who has previously had no problems.

If any of these occur, the person should be seen by a doctor. It used to be thought that neck X-rays could identify whether or not the joint is unstable. However, recent investigations have shown this is not always the case. Coaches are recommended to take into consideration the risks involved in their sport in competition and training in relation to performers with or without down's syndrome, and take precautions as necessary to reduce any possibility of neck injury. This may mean consulting with the sport-specific governing body, parents or guardians of performers with down's syndrome and, of course, the performers themselves. It is recommended that coaches read *Atlanto-Axial Instability among People with Down's Syndrome* which can be obtained from the Down's Syndrome Association (address in Appendix E). The leaflet contains the following quote:

> *Life for everyone is not without risk. It is for the individual to decide what risks are acceptable for their children or for themselves. We all have to compromise in our day-to-day lives as we balance freedom to take part in and enjoy life's activities against the risk of possible injury.*
>
> *Dr Jennifer Dennis*
> *Medical Adviser to the Down's Syndrome Association*

Hearing impairment

Damage to the ear can result in hearing loss of one of the following types:

- **Conductive deafness** which is described as sound not being transmitted well to the inner ear. Winnick (1990) likens it to a radio being turned down low. The sounds are faint but there is no distortion. Conductive deafness can sometimes be corrected.

- **Sensori-neural deafness** which can be likened to a radio not being tuned in properly (Winnick 1990). There is distortion to the sound as well as the volume. Sound messages are disrupted on their way to the brain.

- **Mixed conductive and sensori-neural deafness.** Some people have a mixed conductive and sensori-neural loss.

Other useful terminology associated with hearing impairment include the following:

- Deafness – a hearing loss which makes it impossible to understand speech through hearing alone, even if a hearing aid is used. There is usually a need for another means of communication such as lip-reading or signing.

- Hearing loss – refers to any problems with understanding normal speech.

- Hard of hearing – this makes the understanding of speech difficult but not impossible.

- Residual hearing – residual hearing is the speech that the individual can understand while wearing a hearing aid.

Hydrocephalus

This is a swelling of the brain caused by a blockage. In everyone, cerebrospinal fluid (CSF) is produced constantly inside each of the four ventricles of the brain. It normally flows from one ventricle to the next, then out over the surface of the brain and down the spinal cord where it is absorbed into the bloodstream. If the drainage pathways are obstructed, CSF accumulates in the ventricles inside the brain causing them to swell.

Excess pressure caused by the blockage can be relieved by the insertion of a valve or shunt, which drains excess fluid into the abdominal or heart cavities. Most people born with spina bifida also have hydrocephalus but it can occur independently at birth and later in life. Coaches should be aware of performers complaining of headaches and nausea as this may mean there is a shunt blockage or the CSF drainage pathways are obstructed. Medical advice should be sought if this is suspected. Coaches are recommended to contact ASBAH (Association for Spina Bifida and Hydrocephalus) and ask for their leaflet *What is Hydrocephalus?* for more information (address in Appendix E).

Learning disability

A learning disability is a condition in which the brain does not develop as fast or as fully as it should.

The degree of learning disability can vary enormously. It can be caused by several factors but the four most common result from:

- a genetic (inherited) characteristic such as in people with Down's syndrome

- an infection, such as meningitis

- a trauma, for example from an accident at birth, a road traffic accident or a head injury

- social effects, for example as a result of pre-natal influences such as drugs, alcohol, smoking, malnutrition and pollution.

The damage to the brain can cause delay in physical, social, intellectual and emotional development. The performer functions at a level which is less than his/her chronological age. A learning disability cannot be cured but in many instances, a well structured educational programme, including sports activities, before, during and after school, can help an individual reach his/her full potential. However, most individuals will need some sort of support to some degree throughout their lives. Performers with a learning disability have a normal life expectancy but are more likely to suffer from epilepsy and other conditions which can affect life expectancy.

Muscular dystrophy

This refers to a number of conditions that affect the muscle fibres and cause muscle weakness. All the dystrophies are inherited. The most common type of muscular dystrophy is **duchenne** which is inherited by boys from their mothers. It is rare for girls to inherit the condition, although they can become carriers. Muscular dystrophy is a progressive, degenerative condition which means that an individual's strength and ability will decline over time. Adjustments will therefore be needed to individual training programmes. The muscles of the heart and chest are affected, as well as those of the back and limbs. There is usually a progression from walking to using a manual, then a battery powered wheelchair. There may be a shortened life expectancy. For more information, contact the Muscular Dystrophy Group of Great Britain and Northern Ireland (address in Appendix E).

Multiple sclerosis

MS symptoms result from damage to myelin, the protective coating surrounding all the nerve fibres in the brain, the eye and the spinal cord. Myelin works like insulating cable, helping to conduct messages quickly and efficiently between the brain or spinal cord and the rest of the body. When myelin is damaged, messages are slower or distorted or do not get through at all. Damaged areas of myelin are known as plaques or lesions.

The nature of MS symptoms depends on where damage occurs to myelin in the central nervous system. Damage to nerves responsible for movement can result in poor coordination. Damage to nerves responsible for sensation can result in numbness or tingling. There may be nothing wrong with actual muscles or senses; it is simply that not all the right messages are getting through

Regular exercise is important to people with MS, but should be taken according to individual capabilities as over-exertion could cause fatigue which could exacerbate the condition. For more information, contact the Multiple Sclerosis Society (address in Appendix E).

Spinal cord injuries[1]

The spinal cord is the body's means of communication. Running through the bony vertebral (spinal) column, it is made up of nerves which carry messages between the brain and all other parts of the body. A healthy spinal cord will allow uninterrupted communication along its entire system. The sensory nerves will relay messages of feeling and sensation to the brain which will in turn convert them, via motor nerves, into responses such as movements.

If the spinal cord becomes damaged somewhere along its length the ability to communicate between the brain and the body parts below that point becomes diminished or impossible. If there is an incomplete lesion[2] of the spinal cord, some or all sensation and movement may be retained below the point of injury. A complete lesion will result in total paralysis below the point of injury.

---

1   The information pertaining to spinal problems has been adapted by kind permission of *Back-Up Trust,* address in Appendix E.
2   Lesion is the point of damage.

Paraplegia results from a broken back. There will be partial or total paralysis from the chest or waist (depending on the level of lesion) downwards. With normal upper body power and function, a paraplegic can usually lead an independent lifestyle.

Tetraplegia results from a broken neck. There will be partial or total paralysis of all four limbs. Very high lesions will also affect the diaphragm. In such cases breathing can only be maintained by external mechanical ventilators or by a pacing device. Tetraplegics will usually be highly dependent on others for their care.

In both paraplegia and tetraplegia, control of bodily function (eg bladder, bowels, sexual function) will also be affected.

Spinal injury occurs in several ways but mainly through trauma (ie injury) to the fragile nerve fibres of the spinal cord. The most common causes being road traffic accidents and sporting injuries. Less common, though equally damaging, are viral infections, viruses, growths and diseases of the spinal cord. Figure 2 shows the spinal column with its various sections and landmarks.

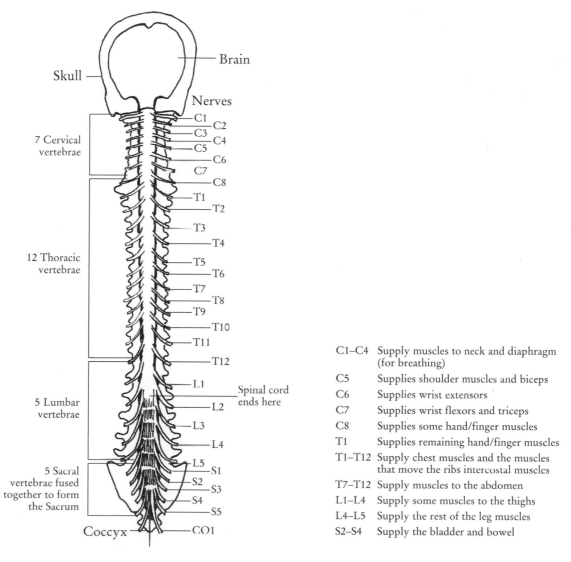

C1–C4	Supply muscles to neck and diaphragm (for breathing)
C5	Supplies shoulder muscles and biceps
C6	Supplies wrist extensors
C7	Supplies wrist flexors and triceps
C8	Supplies some hand/finger muscles
T1	Supplies remaining hand/finger muscles
T1–T12	Supply chest muscles and the muscles that move the ribs intercostal muscles
T7–T12	Supply muscles to the abdomen
L1–L4	Supply some muscles to the thighs
L4–L5	Supply the rest of the leg muscles
S2–S4	Supply the bladder and bowel

Figure 2: The spinal column
Reproduced with kind permission from Back-Up Trust

Post poliomyelitis impairment

This condition results from a viral infection affecting the spinal cord leading to temporary or permanent paralysis. The severity and location of paralysis varies between individuals and depends on how the spinal cord has been affected. Performers who have had poliomyelitis differ from performers who have spinal cord injuries in the following ways:

- Sensation is retained so pain can be felt in the limbs.

- Bowel and bladder control is retained.

- They are aware of the position of their limbs as messages can be sent back from the limbs to the brain.

Spina bifida

Spina Bifida happens very early in pregnancy, when the spine and brain are being formed. It is a fault in the development of the spine, when one or more vertebrae fail to close properly, leaving a gap.

This means the vitally important spinal cord and nerves are likely to be damaged, often resulting in paralysis below the level of the fault. Walking may be difficult or impossible. There may also be the problem of incontinence.

The severity depends very much on where the spina bifida is and the amount of nerve damage.

Coaches are recommended to contact ASBAH (Association for Spina Bifida and Hydrocephalus) and ask for their leaflet *What is Spina Bifida?* for more information (address in Appendix E).

Visual impairment

For the purposes of this pack, the term visual impairment encompasses those people who are totally blind as well as those who are partially sighted. There are many causes of visual impairment which can generally be categorised as:

- congenital (present from birth)

- acquired (occurring after birth as a result of accident, disease or old age).

Whether visual impairment has resulted from a congenital or an acquired cause, the major physical outcome is damage to one or more of the following:

- The eye itself.

- Muscles of the eye.

- Central nervous system.

- Occipital lobe of the brain (the centre for visual identification).

- Optic nerves which relay information from the eye to the brain.

There are various types of impairment:

- Total blindness – the inability to recognise objects or contours in any direction or at any distance.

- Light perception – the ability to distinguish a strong light when it is about one metre from the eye.

- Residual vision – an individual's remaining available vision.

Do not make assumptions about a performer's visual impairment and abilities. Ask the performer to establish the level of vision and any factors that may affect it.

Further Information on Medical Conditions

Asthma

Asthma is a condition in which the breathing tubes or airways (bronchial tubes) in the lungs are narrowed. This happens because the:

- muscles in the airways contract to cause a spasm
- lining of the airway becomes swollen and inflamed
- mucus production is increased in the airways.

These can result from:

- a virus infection such as influenza
- exercise
- sudden changes in temperature
- house dust mite
- an allergic reaction (eg to some food substances, smoke, animal fur)
- excitement and stress
- fumes such as glue or paint.

Although the symptoms of asthma vary from individual to individual, the most common symptoms are coughing, wheezing, chest tightness, difficulty in breathing and tiredness.

Management and treatment

There are three basic approaches:

1 **Medication** – symptoms of exercise induced asthma may be prevented by taking reliever medication prior to exercise – this cannot guarantee that symptoms will be prevented.

2 **Avoidance of trigger factors** – it is relatively easy to avoid some trigger factors (such as smoke or animal fur) but in some cases they may be impossible to avoid, for example, exercise induced asthma. Avoiding exercise may prove detrimental to the overall fitness of the individual. Being physically fit can be of great benefit to asthmatics as exercise improves lung capacity.

3 **Physical preparation** – warm-up exercises such as several 30 second sprints over 5–10 minutes before vigorous games may protect the lungs for an hour or so.

Dealing with an acute asthma attack

1 Encourage the athlete to use the prescribed reliever medication as soon as possible.

2 Never encourage the person to run through an attack.

3 Be aware of the athlete's medical pro forma for details of medication.

4 Help the athlete to relax by keeping calm and avoiding panic. The anxiety caused by the athlete feeling breathless may be made worse if those around are not calm.

5 The medication should take effect in 10–15 minutes. If symptoms do not respond after 2–3 doses of medication, seek medical help immediately.

As a coach working with a performer who has asthma, it is useful to establish how the individual manages his/her condition, as each individual will have his/her own strategy. It is recommended that coaches obtain a copy of *Exercise and Asthma* available from the National Asthma Campaign (address in Appendix E).

Diabetes

Diabetes is a condition in which the body, because of the lack of hormone insulin, is not able to absorb sugar and starch properly. Insulin is one of the hormones that regulates blood glucose concentration levels. It is also involved in the chemical reaction that allows glucose to enter the cells of the body. The glucose in the blood is important as it is essential for normal brain function. If there is not enough insulin, the body cannot use the energy that is contained in the food that is eaten. When this happens, glucose builds up in the blood and overflows into the urine. Generally, injections of insulin help individuals maintain normal blood glucose concentration levels.

Some individuals acquire diabetes later in life – this is known as non-insulin dependent diabetes. It can be managed by healthy eating or a combination of healthy eating and appropriate medication and sometimes with insulin injections. If a performer has diabetes, he/she can check his/her blood glucose levels by the following procedures:

• Placing a drop of blood on a special chemically impregnated strip and comparing the colour of the strip manually against the strip container.

• Using a blood glucose metre.

If a performer with diabetes is over-exerted, there is a possibility of experiencing a diabetic reaction or drifting into a diabetic coma. There are two forms of diabetic reaction:

Hyperglycaemia (high blood glucose levels) which can occur:

- if not enough insulin is taken
- if lots of sweet foods with rapidly absorbed sugar are eaten
- as a result of illness.

The signs are:

- excessive urination and thirst
- itching skin
- slow healing of sores and cuts
- blurred or reduced vision
- increased appetite with weight loss
- easy tiring, drowsiness or fatigue
- headaches
- nausea and sluggishness
- coma.

Hypoglycaemia (low blood glucose levels) which can occur if:

- too much insulin is taken
- meals or snacks are missed
- unplanned physical activities are undertaken.

The signs are:

- hunger, pallor, weakness and perspiration
- mental confusion
- the shakes
- nausea
- changes in behaviour – unusual aggression or quietness
- loss of balance
- blurred or jumpy vision
- sleepiness
- coma.

It is unusual for performers to lapse into a coma as symptoms are usually recognised before this. If any of these symptoms are observed, deal with the performer in the way described in the following panel.

Dealing with diabetics in emergency situations
Usually the diabetic athlete will be able to tell you he/she requires rest, and over-exertion can be avoided. If this does not occur and the athlete collapses, move to a safe place and keep him/her warm.

If the athlete is conscious:

- give tablets if available (eg Dextrose or the equivalent) or sugar if not (eg a sweet drink (not a diet drink), barley sugar or about seven jelly beans)

- give some complex carbohydrate foods next (eg sandwiches or half a dozen cracker biscuits)

- observe the athlete carefully until recovery is complete or help arrives.

If unconscious (fortunately this is rare):

- place the athlete in the coma position and get medical help immediately; in the case of a child and if appropriate, the messenger should also contact the parents

- do not give the athlete fluid or tablets as this may cause choking; if available, use Hypostop (a form of jelly that can be rubbed into the side of the gums)

- observe the athlete until medical assistance arrives.

There are several hazards and contraindications of the involvement of diabetics in physical activity programmes.

Hazards

- Successful diabetes management routines should be established before an exercise programme is started. If exercise occurs with a lack of insulin in the blood, the blood sugar will rise during exercise and hyperglycaemia may develop. Newly diagnosed diabetics or those having difficulty managing their condition, should be cautious when beginning a training programme.

- An exercise ECG is usually arranged for diabetics past the age of 40 years or if the duration of the diabetes exceeds 25 years. Diabetics are two or three times more likely to suffer heart and large artery disease than non-diabetics. Consequently, a functional test of their circulation and exercise capacity should be administered. The results of the tests are useful in deciding if their exercise programme should be supervised and for the writing of an exercise prescription.

- Cotton socks as feet can become more easily damaged on performers with diabetes.

Contraindications

- Diabetes is known as the great imitator because it can imitate a number of other medical conditions. In the long-term, diabetes can affect almost every organ of the body and complications are many and varied, some of which are listed below:

  - Microangiopathy – vascular disease (ie hardening of the larger and the smaller blood vessels).

  - Arteriosclerosis – degenerative changes in the arteries occur prematurely in diabetics.

  - Diabetic retinopathy – a retinal vascular disease which can culminate in haemorrhaging (bleeding) within the retina and blindness if diabetes is not controlled.

  - Peripheral vascular disease (ie poor circulation in the extremities, in particular the feet).

  - Neuropathy (ie poor sensation, particularly in the feet) – this condition may result in an individual being unaware of injuries and consequently the need to treat the injury.

  - Infection – poor control of diabetes can lead to greater risk of infection generally.

In most instances, diabetes presents no real problems to performers as long as a balance is maintained between the:

- diet
- type and amount of medication
- timing of meals
- time of peak insulin activity
- intensity of exercise
- time when the insulin injection is taken – may be dispensed more quickly if injection site is involved in activity.

It is important for the individual performers to establish a routine to manage the condition and that as a coach, you are aware of this and what to do in an emergency. Diabetes UK can supply information on all aspects of diabetes including diet and hypoglycaemia (address in Appendix E).

Epilepsy

Epilepsy is a tendency to have recurrent seizures. They may take many forms, differing from one person to another but it is always due to an altered chemical state within the brain. In many cases, the causes of epilepsy are unknown but seizures can be caused by factors such as:

- brain damage

- tumours

- injury or infection.

There are certain factors which may trigger seizures in a susceptible person, such as stress, hormonal changes, lack of sleep, anxiety and lack of food.

There are several kinds of seizures – the most common are:

- generalised absence (used to be called petit mal); the person looks blank and stares for a few seconds, then normal activity will continue

- generalised tonic-clonic (previously called grand mal); a common sequence would be stiffening of the body, convulsions, possible blue colour around the mouth and the seizure could last for a few minutes

- complex partial – this involves an altered state of awareness; the person may display strange behaviour or inappropriate actions and may be confused afterwards.

The majority of people with epilepsy have their seizures controlled by anti-epileptic medication. The best way of understanding epilepsy is to speak to the performer concerned and establish how he/she manages his/her seizures and what action he/she would expect you to take. Each person's epilepsy is different. The following panels provide some additional guidance. Coaches who require more information are recommended to contact the British Epilepsy Association (address in Appendix E).

Guidance for coping with a seizure

- No restraints should be applied.

- Do not put anything in the person's mouth.

- The seizure should be allowed to take its course.

- Make the environment safe (ie place a jumper under the person's head, loosen tight clothing, remove electrical goods, sharp objects, glasses). In water environments (ie depending on numbers for lifting and closeness to land, jetties, boats), the athlete should be lifted out of the water. If this is not possible, try to support the head above the water. Appropriate buoyancy aids should help and probably keep the individual safer in the water.

- When the seizure has subsided, turn the person onto his/her side and allow saliva to flow from the mouth and keep the airway open, try to keep the person warm and calm, stay with him/her and keep him/her company. Allow the person to rest and monitor his/her airway, breathing and circulation (ABC).

- Seek medical assistance immediately (ie call an ambulance) if:

  - a seizure lasts for more than ten minutes or longer than usual for that person

  - seizures continue one after another without recovery in between

  - the person has sustained an injury during the seizure (eg hit head)

  - the person does not have a history of epilepsy (ie it is the first seizure).

- Commence cardiopulmonary resuscitation (CPR) if the person is not breathing normally one minute after the seizure is over.

General hints for coaching athletes with convulsive disorders

- Secure a medical report on all athletes (ie develop a medical pro forma for all athletes to complete).

- Ask for any information regarding medication and precautionary action and do not disturb the medication schedule.

- Check the athlete's medical needs – particularly if you are travelling for competitions or training camps.

- Remember, fatigue can induce seizures. Develop an appropriate monitoring system between you and the athlete to try to avoid situations where the athlete becomes overly distressed.

- Monitor athletes with epilepsy closely during cool-down periods as seizures are more likely to occur in this period rather than during the activity itself.

- Avoid rapidly changing environments, flickering lights, flashing lights and strobe lights for people who have photosensitive epilepsy.

- During aquatic activities, it is essential the athlete is supervised at all times.

- Take all precautions with those whose seizures are not medically controlled.

- Be aware that alcohol can increase the likelihood of a seizure occurring.

- Some females are more prone to seizures during menstruation.

- Be aware of the information in the previous panel.

Haemophilia

Haemophilia is a blood condition in which an essential clotting factor is either partly or completely missing. This causes a person with haemophilia to bleed for longer than normal. Cuts and grazes are not great problems as a little pressure and a plaster are usually enough to stop bleeding. The main problem is internal bleeding into joints, muscles and soft tissues. Haemophilia is a lifelong inherited genetic condition, which affects females as carriers and males who inherit the condition. About a third of new diagnoses are where there is no previous family history. It appears world-wide and occurs in all racial groups. About 6,000 people are affected with haemophilia in the UK. There are two types of haemophilia, the most common being haemophilia A, in which Factor VIII is lacking. In haemophilia B, Factor IX is lacking.

People with severe haemophilia can experience spontaneous bleeding usually into the joints. If left untreated these bleeds cause acute pain and severe joint damage leading to disability. Bleeding episodes have caused difficulties with education and employment, as well as mobility problems for many who have been crippled by the effects of regular bleeding into joints.

Classification Systems

You were introduced to the complexities of classification in Chapter Five. Classification is primarily divided into sensory, physical and intellectual impairment. Within the first two categories, there are sub-divisions based upon the nature of the sport and the functional ability to perform it. Not all disabilities compete in the Paralympic events.

Classification systems are constantly being refined by the international and national disabilities sports organisations as medical and sports technical collaboration grows. The 1996 *Atlanta Paralympic Games General and Functional Classification Guide* is nearly 200 A4 pages long. Each of the 19 paralympic sports has its own section describing the classification of performers eligible for competition.

Athletes are usually grouped together according to level of functional ability and not according to impairment group. However in some cases, it is necessary for athletes to be grouped together according to their impairment group.

In the archery competition at the 1996 Atlanta Paralympic games, members of the international sports organisations were classified according to functional ability, regardless of impairment group. Blind and visually impaired performers and those with a learning disability were not included, as they do not compete in archery at Paralympic level.

This example shows how athletes with different disabilities are grouped together functionally. However, this may not always be possible. For example at Atlanta in the swimming events, visually impaired swimmers competed amongst themselves and not against swimmers with other impairments. Within this group, swimmers were classified further according to level of sight.

There is further classification for competitors with learning disabilities as well as competitors with physical disabilities, who can be grouped together according to level of functional ability and performance.

Performers who are deaf or hard of hearing

Performers are divided into male and female categories.

Performers with a learning disability

Since the majority of competitive opportunities available to athletes with learning disability nationally and internationally offer a single open class to both men and women, no classification system is required.

In order to compete, athletes must prove their eligibility by providing evidence they have a learning disability (intellectual disability/mental handicap) against a set of criteria laid down by the International Sports Federation for Persons with Mental Handicap/Intellectual Disability (INAS-FMH). These criteria are also used nationally but are currently under review.

Some competitive opportunities are organised to offer banded competition enabling performers of similar ability to compete against each other. Banded competition is predominantly used in local and regional competitions to encourage participation. However, opportunities do exist, promoted by Special Olympics, which enable athletes with learning disabilities to participate in banded competitions nationally and internationally. These opportunities are also intended to encourage and reward participation and are not primarily driven by performance.

Please do not let the apparent complexities of the classification system detract from your enthusiasm to coach disabled performers. There are knowledgeable officers within the NDSOs and several NGBs who will be able to guide and advise performers and coaches to the most appropriate line of action.

Brief History of Disabled Sport and Present Structure

It is generally considered that sport for disabled people has developed largely this century with the introduction in 1948 of competition for wheelchair athletes at Stoke Mandeville Hospital, Aylesbury. The first International Wheelchair Games were organised by Sir Ludgwig Guttman, a neurosurgeon, to coincide with the London Olympics. This was done in an attempt to give the Games the same status as the Olympic Games. A deliberate attempt to connect the Olympics and Paralympics (Parallel Olympics) was not made again until 1960 in Rome. Since that time, the Paralympics have been held every four years. Table 3 shows some of the cities and countries which have hosted the Olympic Games.

Table 3: Cities and countries which have hosted the Paralympic Games

Year	City	Country	Olympics
1960	Rome	Italy	Rome
1964	Tokyo	Japan	Tokyo
1968	Tel Aviv	Israel	Mexico
1972	Heidelberg	Germany	Munich
1976	Toronto	Canada	Montreal
1980	Arnhem	Holland	Moscow[1]
1984	Stoke Mandeville and	England	Los Angeles
	Nassau County, New York	USA	
1988	Seoul	Korea	Seoul[2]
1992	Barcelona	Spain	Barcelona
1996	Atlanta	USA	Atlanta
2000	Sydney	Australia	Sydney

1   The Soviet Union, at that time, said it had no disabled citizens and would consequently be unable to hold the Paralympic Games.

2   Seoul is generally acknowledged to be the first, *modern* Paralympics. The Koreans had no background in disability sport and just chose to *parallel* the Olympic arrangements.

The Winter Paralympics are held every four years, the first Games being held in 1990 in France with the 1994 Games being held in Lillehammer in Norway and most recently, the 1998 Games in Nagano, Japan. However, disabled performers have competed in demonstration events in several previous Winter Olympics. Like the Summer Paralympics, the Winter Paralympics are the pinnacle of competition for elite athletes with physical disabilities and the opportunity to compete will arise again at the 2002 event in Salt Lake City.

Initially, the Paralympics only catered for athletes who used wheelchairs but gradually, as the Paralympic movement grew, other classes of athletes began to participate. In 1982 the International Co-ordinating Committee of World Sports Organisation for the Disabled (ICC) was established as a counterpart to the International Olympic Committee. The ICC had four International Federations under its umbrella:

- Cerebral Palsy International Sports and Recreation Association (CP-ISRA)
- International Blind Sports Association (IBSA)
- International Stoke Mandeville Wheelchair Sports Federation (ISMWSF)
- International Sports Organisation for the Disabled (ISOD). This organisation governs amputees as well as Les Autres Performers.

In 1992 the ICC was restructured and became the International Paralympic Committee (IPC). The International Sports Organisations organise international competition for their own specific disability groups. Their national counterparts organise national level competition for their own specific disability groups. Some able-bodied national and international sports federations are beginning to organise and include events for disability in their programmes. For more information, contact the national disability sports organisations (NDSO) – the address can be found in Appendix E.

As the Paralympic Movement has developed over the years, performers with learning disability have been integrated into events. The International Association for Sport for Persons with Mental Handicap (INAS-FMH) is universally recognised as representing the interests of performers with mental handicap/learning disability and is a member of the IPC. As well as working towards the integration of performers with a learning disability into the Paralympics, INAS-FMH has also organised other events, for example, World Championships in athletics, basketball, table tennis, swimming and football. INAS-FMH worked with the Sydney Paralympics in 2000 to offer a full programme of competition to performers with a learning disability.

The Special Olympics movement was founded in 1968 by Eunice Kennedy Shriver to enable people with a learning disability to compete together. The emphasis of the Special Olympics movement is on giving individuals the opportunity to compete in the sports of their choice, regardless of ability, each individual athlete being matched to other athletes of similar ability for competition. The emphasis is on participation.

The World Games for the Deaf have been held regularly since the first games in 1924 in Paris. The games are held every four years in the year following the Olympic year. The games are not only concerned with competition but are also a celebration of deaf culture. For more information on the development of sport for particular disability groups, contact the appropriate NDSO (addresses in Appendix E).

Development of the Paralympic movement

1948   First competition for athletes with a disability, Stoke Mandeville
1952   First international competition for athletes with a spinal cord lesion
1976   Amputees included in international games
1980   Blind athletes and the Les Autres group join the disability sports movement
1984   Athletes with cerebral palsy compete in Paralympics
1988   First true *Paralympic Games*
1992   Athletes with learning difficulties included (separate event)
1996   Further integration of athletes with learning difficulties.

Organisations that coordinate sport for people with disabilities

National coordination of international multi-disciplinary competition/activity

- British Paralympic Association (BPA). Emphasis on elite performance.

UK/home country sports associations

- United Kingdom Sports Association for People with Learning Disability (UKSAPLD)

- Disability Sport Cymru and the Federation of Sports Associations for the Disabled.

- Scottish Disability Sport

- Disability Sport NI

- English Federation of Disability Sport.

National disability sports organisations

- British Wheelchair Sports Foundation (BWSF)

- Cerebral Palsy Sport (CP Sport)

- British Amputee and Les Autres Sports Association (BALASA)

- British Blind Sport (BBS)

- British Deaf Sports Council (BDSC)

- English Sports Association for People with a Learning Disability (ESAPLD)

} Emphasis on development of performance.

- Mini Olympics

- Special Olympics

- Gateway/Mencap.

} Emphasis on participation.

National sport-specific disability organisations

For example:

- Great Britain Wheelchair Basketball Association

- Riding for the Disabled Association

- English Table Tennis Association for the Disabled

- RYA Sailability

- Great Britain Wheelchair Rugby Association

- British Tennis Foundation.

English Federation of Disability Sport

Following two years of discussions between the various National Disability Sports Organisations, governing bodies of sport representatives and other agencies, the English Federation of Disability Sport (EFDS) was formed in 1998 and is now the principal agency responsible for the coordinated development of sport for disabled people in England.

The EFDS has the support and direct involvement of all major disability sports organisations and, working through new or established regional structures for disability sport, will promote a corporate approach at national and regional level to determine priorities and the implementation of work programmes.

The aim of the EFDS is to provide a 'first stop shop' on disability sport issues and priority will be given to work aimed at:

- increasing effectiveness of the current structure in disability sport
- promoting the inclusion of disabled people within mainstream programmes of national governing bodies of sport, local authorities and other providers
- accessing Lottery Revenue Programmes and Sport England Programmes
- raising the profile of sport for disabled people
- creating networks and improving communications.

A key element of the new federation is its regional structure and in each of the ten Sport England regions a forum or federation has been established to support the work of the national organisation at regional level. In order to support the work of the Regional Federations, Disability Sport Managers have been appointed in all the regions with varying additional staffing structures.

Useful Addresses and Contacts

For the UK

Association for Spina Bifida and Hydrocephalus (ASBAH)
ASBAH House, 42 Park Road, Peterborough PE1 2UQ
Tel: 01733-555988, Fax: 01733-555985
E-mail: postmaster@asbah.org, Website: www.asbah.org

Back-Up Trust
The Business Village, Broomhill Road, Wandsworth, London SW18 4JQ
Tel: 020-8875 1805, Fax: 020-8870 3619, E-mail: admin@backuptrust.org.uk,
Website: www.backuptrust.org.uk

British Amputee and Les Autres Sports Association (BALASA)
5 Bells Farm Close, Brandwood, Birmingham, B14 5QP
Tel: 0121-605 9549

British Blind Sport (BBS)
4–6 Victoria Terrace, Leamington Spa, Warwickshire CV31 3AB
Tel: 08700-789000 or 08700-789001, E-mail: info@britishblindsport.org.uk
Website: www.britishblindsport.org.uk

British Deaf Sports Council
7 Bridge Street, Otley, West Yorkshire LS21 1BQ
Voice: 01943-850214, DCT: 01943-850081, Fax: 01943-850828

Diabetes UK
10 Parkway, London NW1 7AA
Tel: 020-7424 1000, Fax: 020-7424 1001, E-mail: info@diabetes.org.uk,
Website: www.diabetes.org.uk

Epilepsy Action
New Anstey House, Gate Way Drive, Yeadon, Leeds LS19 7NW
Tel: 0113-210 8800, Fax: 0113 391-0300, E-mail: epilepsy@epilepsy.org.uk
Website: www. epilepsy.org.uk

British Paralympic Association
Norwich Union Building, 9th floor, 69 Park Lane, Croydon, Surrey, CR9 1BG
Tel: 020-7662 8882, Fax: 020-7662 8310, E-mail: info@paralympics.org.uk,
Website: www.paralympics.org.uk

British Wheelchair Sports Foundation
Guttmann Road, Stoke Mandeville, Buckinghamshire HP21 9PP
Tel: 01926-395995, Fax: 01926-424171, E-mail: enquiries@britishwheelchairsports.org
Website: www.britishwheelchairsports.org

Central Council for Physical Recreation
Francis House, Francis Street, London SW1P 1DE
Tel: 020-7854 8500, Fax: 020-7854 8501, E-mail: info@ccpr.org.uk, Website: www.ccpr.org.uk

C P Sport
Suite 32, Trent Bridge Cricket Centre, Notts County Cricket Club Ltd, Trent Bridge,
Nottingham NG2 6AG
Tel: 0115-982 5352 or 0115-982 5358, Fax: 0115-981 5484, E-mail: info@cpsport.org,
Website: www.cpsport.org

Downs Syndrome Association
155 Mitcham Road, London SW17 9PG
Tel: 020-8682 4001, Fax: 020-8682 4012, E-mail: info@downs-syndrome.org.uk,
Website: www.dsa-uk.com

Friends for Young Deaf People
120a Abbet Street, Nuneaton, CV11 5BX
Tel: 024-7663 1517, Fax: 024-7664 1517, Minicom: 024-7632 8083

MENCAP
MENCAP 123 Golden Lane, London EC1Y 0RT
Tel: 020-7454 0454, Fax: 020-7696 5540, E-mail: information@mencap.org.uk, Website:
www.mencap.org.uk

Multiple Sclerosis Society
372 Edgeware Rd, London, NW2 6ND
Tel: 020-8438 0700, Fax: 020-8438 0701, E-mail: info@mssociety.org.uk,
Website: www.mssociety.org.uk

Muscular Dystrophy Campaign
7–11 Prescott Place, London SW4 6BS
Tel: 020-7720 8055, Fax: 020-7498 0670, E-mail: info@muscular-dystrophy.org,
Website: www.muscular-dystrophy.org

National Asthma Campaign
Providence House, Providence Place, London N1 ONT
Tel: 020-7226 2260, Fax: 020-7704 0740, Website: www.asthma.org.uk

Physically Disabled and Able Bodied
Summit House, Wandle Road, Croydon CR0 1DF
Tel: 020-8667 9443, Fax: 020-8681 1399, E-mail: info@phabengland.org.uk,
Website: www.phabengland.org.uk

Royal National Institute for the Deaf (RNID)
19–23 Featherstone Street, London EC1Y 8SL
Tel: 020-7296 8000, Fax: 020-7296 8199, Textphone: 020-7296 8001
E-mail: informationline@rnid.org.uk, Website: www.rnid.org.uk

United Kingdom Sports Association for People with Learning Disability (UKSAPLD)
Ground Floor, Leroy House, 436 Essex Rd, London, N1 3QP
Tel: 020-7354 1030 Fax: 020-7354 2593, E-mail: office@uksapld.freeserve.co.uk

For England

Regional managers – English Federation of Disability Sport[1]

East	The Hemel Hempstead Sports Centre Park Road, Hemel Hempstead Hertfordshire, HP1 1JS	Tel: 01442-228791 Fax: 01442-228757 E-mail: east@efds.co.uk
East Midlands	Sports Development Centre Loughborough LE11 3TU	Tel: 01509-228 030 Fax: 01509-223 995 Minicom: 01509-240 655 E-mail: eastmidlands@efds.co.uk
London	London Sports Forum for Disabled People Ground Floor, Leroy House 436 Essex Road London N1 3QP	Tel: 020-7354 8666 Fax: 020-7354 8787 Minicom: 020-7354 9554 E-mail: lsf@disabilitysport.freeserve.co.uk
North	House of Sport (SDO Centre) University of Durham, South End House South Road, Durham DH1 3TG	Tel: 0191-374 8308 Fax: 0191-374 8302 Minicom: 0191-374 8311 E-mail: north@efds.co.uk
North West	Leisure Services Dept, Wyvern House The Drumber, Winsford, Northwich CW7 1AH	Tel: 01606 867 863 Fax: 01606-862 100 E-mail: northwest@efds.co.uk
South East		Tel: 01277-849229 E-mail: southeast@efds.co.uk
South West	Bristol Leisure Services, Colston House, Colston Street Bristol BS1 5AQ	Tel: 0117-922 2717 Fax: 0117-922 3735 Minicom: 0117 922-2717 E-mail: southwest@efds.co.uk
West Midlands	House of Sport, University College Worcester, Henwick Grove, Worcester WR2 6AJ	Tel: 01905-855 429 Fax: 01905-855 426 Minicom: 01905-855 448 E-mail: westmidlands@efds.co.uk
Yorkshire	Federation of Disability Sports Organisations, Unit 9, Milner Way, Ossett, West Yorkshire WF5 9JN	Tel: 01924-279 305 Fax: 01924-280 232 E-mail: staff@fdso.co.uk

Disability Sport England (Events Agency)
National Head Office, Unit 4G, N17 Studios, 784–788 High Road, Tottenham, London,
N17 0DA, Tel: 020-8801 4466, Fax: 020-8801 6644,
E-mail: info@dse.org.uk, Website: www.disabilitysport.org.uk.

1   Correct December 2001.

Sport England
16 Upper Woburn Place, London WC1H 0QP
Tel: 020-7273 1500, Fax: 020-7383 5740, E-mail: info@sportengland.org,
Website: www.sportengland.org

English Sports Association for People with Learning Disabilities
Unit 9, Milner Way, Ossett, West Yorkshire WF5 9JN
Tel: 01924-267555, Fax: 01924-267666, E-mail: info@esapld.co.uk,
Website: www.esapld.co.uk

For Northern Ireland

Disability Sport NI
Unit 10, Ormeau Business Park, 8 Cromac Avenue, Belfast, BT7 2JA
Tel: 028-9050 8255, Fax: 028-9050 8256, Textphone: 028-9050 8254
E-mail: email@dsni.co.uk, Website: www.dsni.co.uk

Disability Action
Portside Business Park, 189 Airport Road West, Belfast, BT3 9ED
Tel: 028-9029 7880, Fax: 028-902 7881, Textphone: 028-9029 7882
E-mail: information@disabilityaction.org, Website: www.disabilityaction.org

Northern Ireland Sports Council
House of Sport, Upper Malone Road, Belfast BT9 5LA
Tel: 028-9038 1222, Fax: 028-9068 2757, E-mail: info@sportscouncil-ni.org.uk,
Website: www.sportni.org

For Wales

Disability Sport Cymru
Wales National Sports Centre, Sophia Gardens, Cardiff, CF11 9SW
Tel: 029-2030 0525/6, E-mail: fsad.wales@business.ntl.com

Sports Council for Wales
Sophia Gardens, Cardiff CF11 9SW
Tel: 029-2030 0500, Fax: 029-2030 0600, E-mail: scw@scw.co.uk,
Website: www.sports-council-wales.co.uk

Welsh Sports Association for the Disabled
21 Keir Hardy Terrace, Swffryd Crumlin, Newport, NP11 5EJ
Tel: 01495-248861

For Scotland

Scottish Disability Sport
Fife Sports Institute, Viewfield Road, Glenrothes, Fife KY6 2RB
Tel: 01592-415700, Fax: 01592-415710, E-mail: ssadsds@aol.com,
Website: www.scottishdisabilitysport.com

sportscotland
Caledonia House, South Gyle, Edinburgh EH12 9DQ
Tel: 0131-317 7200 Fax: 0131-317 7202,
E-mail: library@sportscotland.org.uk, Website: www.sportscotland.org.uk

sports coach UK Workshops and Resources

Recommended **scUK** workshops and resources (complimentary with the corresponding workshop) include:

scUK Workshop	Resource
Analysing your Coaching	Analysing your Coaching (home study)
Coaching Children and Young People	Coaching Young Performers
Coaching Disabled Performers	Coaching Disabled Performers (home study)
Coaching Methods and Communication	The Successful Coach
Fitness and Training	Physiology and Performance
Fuelling Performers	Fuelling Performers
Goal-setting and Planning	Planning Coaching Programmes (home study)
Good Practice and Child Protection	Protecting Children (home study)
Improving Practices and Skill	Improving Practices and Skill
Injury Prevention and Management	Sports Injury
Motivation and Mental Toughness	Motivation and Mental Toughness
Observation, Analysis and Video	Observation, Analysis and Video
Equity in Your Coaching	Equity in Your Coaching

Details of all **scUK** resources are available from:

Coachwise 1st4sport
Chelsea Close
Off Amberley Road
Armley
Leeds
LS12 4HP
Tel: 0113-201 5555
Fax: 0113-231 9606
E-mail: enquiries@1st4sport.com
Website: www.1st4sport.com

scUK also produce a technical journal – **Faster, Higher, Stronger (FHS)** and an information update service for coaches **(sports coach update)**. Details of these services are available from:

sports coach UK
114 Cardigan Road
Headingley
Leeds
LS6 3BJ
Tel: 0113-274 4802
Fax: 0113-275 5019
E-mail: coaching@sportscoachuk.org
Website: www.sportscoachuk.org

For direct bookings on **scUK** workshops at Premier Coaching Centres, please contact:

Workshop Booking Centre
Chelsea Close
Off Amberley Road
Armley
Leeds
LS12 4HP
Tel: 0845-601 3054
Fax: 0113-231 9606

For details of all **scUK** workshops, running in your area, contact your nearest Regional Training Unit (RTU) or home countries office. RTU details are available on the **scUK** website.

Other Workshops

There are a number of workshops available from other organisations, which may be of use to anyone involved in coaching disabled performers. Details are available direct from the organisations, see Appendix E for contact details. Accompanying resources may be available either through attendance or for general sale.

English Federation of Disability Sport (EFDS)

- Coaching Disabled Footballers (a workshop for football coaches)

- Including Disabled Pupils in Physical Education (a workshops for teachers)

- Protecting Disabled Children and Adults in Sport and Recreation (a workshop for all involved in provision of sport for disabled people, available from Disability Sport England and English Federation of Disability Sport)

- Coaching Disabled Cricketers (a workshop for cricket coaches)

EFDS also publish a book which summarises courses that are available to disabled people wishing to become coaches and those needing technical information on how to coach disabled performers. *Sport and Disabled People* is available direct from EFDS for £3 per copy.

Youth Sport Trust

- Sportsability (a workshop for teachers, coaches and sports leaders delivering TOP programmes in schools and the community, also available from your local education authority/sports development department)

Running Sport

- Running Sport Equity Programme (a training course for governing bodies)

- Opening Up Your Club (a workshop for clubs which will soon be available from Running Sport and EFDS)

- A Club for All (a workshop for clubs which will shortly be available)

National Federation of Gateway Clubs

- The Get Active Programme (a programme dedicated to the promotion of an active lifestyle for those with learning disabilities which is available to those with learning disabilities and those providing them with a service)

References

BAALPE (1989) **Physical education for children with special educational needs in mainstream education.** London, BAALPE. ISBN 1 871228 03 4

De Pauw, KP and Gavron, SJ (1995) **Disability and sport.** Champaign IL, Human Kinetics. ISBN 0 87322 848 0

Downs, P (1995) **Willing and able: PE and sport for young people with disabilities.** Australian Sports Commission

Findlay, B (1944) **Quality and equality in education: the denial of a disability culture** In Ribbins, P and Burridge, E (eds) **Improving education. Promoting quality in our schools.** London, Cassell (*Out of print*)

Goodman, S (ed) (1993) **Coaching athletes with disabilities: general principles.** Australian Sports Commission, PO Box 176 Belconnen, ACT 2616, Australia

sports coach UK (1996) **The successful coach: guidelines for coaching practice.** Leeds, National Coaching Foundation. ISBN 0 947850 16 3

Concise medical dictionary. (1998) Oxford, Oxford University Press, ISBN 0 192 800 752

Wade, B and Moore, M (1996) **Experiencing special education: what young people with special needs can tell us.** Milton Keynes, Open University Press. ISBN 0 335 096 794

Winnick, JP (ed) (1995) **Adapted physical education and sport.** 2nd edition. Champaign IL, Human Kinetics. ISBN 0 87322 579 1

Further Reading

Books

ASA **Teaching of swimming for those with special needs.** ASA Swimming Enterprises

BAALPE (1989) **Physical education for children with special educational needs in mainstream education.** London, BAALPE, ISBN 1 871228 03 4

Blundell, C **Watersports are for everyone.** Royal Yachting Association (01703 629962)

Braggins, A **Trail orienteering.** British Orienteering Federation (01786 841202)

Brown, A **Active games for children with movement problems.** London, Paul Chapman Publishing Ltd (*Out of print*)

Goldberg, B (1995) **Sport and exercise for children with chronic health conditions.** Champaign IL, Human Kinetics. ISBN 0 87322 873 1

Kasser, SL (1995) **Inclusive games movement fun for everyone.** Champaign IL, Human Kinetics ISBN 0 87322 639 9

Kerr A and Stafford I (2003) **How to Coach Disabled People in Sport.** Leeds, **sports coach UK.** ISBN 1 902523 54 7

Lancashire County Council **Lancashire looks at... physical education in the special school.** Lancashire County Council (01772 54868)

Lockette, K and Keys, A (1994) **Conditioning with physical disabilities.** Champaign IL, Human Kinetics. ISBN 0 87322 614 3

Male, J and Thompson, C **The educational implications of disability – a guide for teachers.** London, Radar (020 7250 3222)

Morris, LM and Schulz, L (1989) **Creative play activities for children with disabilities.** Champaign IL, Human Kinetics. ISBN 0 87322 933 9

National Eczema Society **Eczema in schools.** The National Eczema Society (0870 241 3604)

Newman, I **Outdoor activities for all.** Fieldfare Trust (01334 657708)

Nottingham Trent University, Faculty of Education **Practical innovations for nine adapted activities games and sports.** Nottingham Trent University (0115 941 8418)

Pauw, KP and Gavron, SJ (1995) **Disability and sport.** Champaign IL, Human Kinetics. ISBN 0 87322 848 0

Pointer, B **Movement activities for children with learning difficulties.** London, Kingsley Publishers Ltd. ISBN 1 853021 67 9

Powers, MD (2000) **Children with autism.** London, Woodbine House.
ISBN 1 890627 04 6

Reed, L **The Meldreth series.** London, SCOPE (020 7619 7100)

Royal National Institute for the Blind (1994) **Looking into PE: guidelines for teaching PE to children with visual impairment.** London, RNIB. ISBN 1 80901 206 6

Russell, JP **Graded activities for children with motor difficulties.** Cambridge, Cambridge University Press. ISBN 0 521 33852 2 (*Out of print*)

SCOPE **Activities for people with a multiple disability.** London, SCOPE (020 7619 7100)

Sherborne, V **Development movement for children.** Cambridge, Cambridge University Press. ISBN 0 521 379033 2 (*Out of print*)

Smedley, G (1997) **Canoeing for disabled people.** Leicester, British Canoe Union (0115 982 1100)

Strong, T and Le Fevre, D (1995) **Parachute games.** Champaign IL, Human Kinetics. ISBN 0 87322 793 X

Winnick, JP (ed) (1995) **Adapted physical education and sport.** 2nd edition. Champaign IL, Human Kinetics ISBN 0 87322 579 1

Awards

The Duke of Edinburgh Award Scheme (01753-810753)

The Gateway Award National Award Office, East View House, Shooters Hill, Sutton Coldfield, West Midlands B72 1HX (0121-321 1409)

Newspapers and magazines

Access by Design
Centre for Accessible Environments, Nutmeg House, 60 Gainsford Street, London SE1 2NY
Tel: 020-7357 8182, Fax: 020-7357 8183, E-mail: info@cae.org.uk,
Website: www.cae.org.uk

Link
Asbah House, 42 Park Road, Peterborough PE1 2UQ
Tel: 01733-555988, E-mail: tonyb@asbah.org, Website: www.asbah.org

Disability Times
58 Uxbridge Rd, Ealing, London, W5 2TL
Tel: 020-7233 7970, Fax: 020-8566 1208

Remploy News
415 Edgeware Rd, Cricklewood, London NW2 6LR
Tel: 020-8235 0500, Fax: 020-8235 0501, Website: www.remploy.co.uk

Sports Equipment for Disabled People

In recent years the development of equipment designed to enable disabled people to access sport has improved – primarily through research, the sharing of information and collaboration with disabled people and equipment manufacturers. The following organisations can provide information on equipment that exists and how to gain access to it. Disabled Living Centres around the country may also stock certain items of equipment.

Disability Information Trust

The Disability Information Trust is a registered charity that specialises in the assessment and testing of disability equipment and the publication of independent, verified and in-depth information on that equipment. They produce a series of fully illustrated handbooks presenting essential facts and comments on a wide range of products for easier living, with photographs and price guides, details of manufacturers and bright ideas.

The Disability Information Trust
Nuffield Orthopaedic Centre
Headington
Oxford OX3 7LD

Tel: 01865-227592
Fax: 01865-227596
E-mail: news@abilityonline.org.uk
Website: www.abilityonline.org.uk/disability-information_trust.htm

Disabled Living Foundation

The Disabled Living Foundation believe that everybody has the right to be independent and equal, has the power to choose, and to live their life to its fullest potential. Specialist equipment and adaptations can change someone's quality of life and the right equipment can mean the difference between relying on friends and carers, or remaining independent and in control of your own life. The foundation is a leading source of information on disability equipment, day-to-day household gadgets, new technologies and training techniques and aims to provide solutions for many daily tasks and activities, as well as expert, unbiased knowledge on the right kind of equipment and where to find it.

Disabled Living Foundation
380–384 Harrow Road
London
W9 2HU

Helpline: 0845-130 9177
Textphone: 0870-603 9176
E-mail: info@dlf.org.uk
Website: www.dlf.org.uk

Design for Life Centre and Adventure Designs

The Design for Life Centre (DfL) is a self-funding multidisciplinary team working within Brunel University on the research and development of innovative products primarily for the healthcare industry. DfL currently acts as the leading interface between academia and industry in this field and is recognised as unique in its breadth of expertise.

Adventure Designs is a specific programme at DfL which develops outdoor activity equipment in a collaborative manner with disabled people and equipment manufacturers to give greater access to outdoor pursuits like climbing, canoeing and sailing.

Design for Life Centre
Studio 26
Brunel University
Runnymede
Surrey TW20 0JZ

Tel: 01784-433262
Fax: 01784-470880
E-mail: dfl@brunel.ac.uk
Website: www.brunel.ac.uk/research/dfl/home.htm

Remap

A registered charity which utilises volunteer engineers and craftspeople to develop life-enhancing technical aids for individual disabled people which are not available commercially.

Remap
Hazeldene
Ightam
Sevenoaks
Kent
TN15 9AD

Tel: 0845-130 0456
Fax: 0845-130 0789
Website: www.rcmap.org.uk
E-mail: info@remap.org